D1707734

CAN S&Ls

SURVIVE?

THE EMERGING RECOVERY, RESTRUCTURING & REPOSITIONING OF AMERICA'S S&Ls

ANAT BIRD

BANKERS PUBLISHING COMPANY
PROBUS PUBLISHING COMPANY
Chicago, Illinois
Cambridge, England

BANKLINE

ISBN 1-55738-329-4

Printed in the United States of America

BC

1   2   3   4   5   6   7   8   9   0

To my family
who put the right perspective
in my life.

Table of Contents

List of Figures and Tables

Figures

Tables

Introduction:
Can Thrifts Survive?

Much has been said and written about the thrift industry debacle. Many have discussed the root causes of the thrifts' downfall, which range from external factors such as interest rate volatility in a declining economy and misregulation, to internal factors such as poor management, corruption, and fraud. This book will touch upon the underlying causes of the thrift industry's decline and its condition today. However, its primary focus is the future: Is there a future for the thrift business? Is there a healthy core of savings banks and savings and loan associations which have thus far survived the industry's trials and tribulations and will continue to survive in the future? And, if there is such a core, what form will survival take? Will the new thrift industry be much like the old thrift industry, the institutions which financed individual home ownership in America, or will it take new shapes and possibly even lose its identity as a separate industry in years to come?

The answers to these questions will be followed by an examination of successful strategies for survival of individual institutions within the thrift business and the offering of several prescriptions for success to existing thrifts which are looking for a winning formula to establish their future success beyond mere survival.

The thrift industry is in the process of redefining itself. It is in the process of transition. The surviving thrifts will take on many different shapes, some of which may bear little similarity to what the thrift used to be twenty-five years ago. The battle for strategic identity that the thrifts are waging resulted from the elimination of their historical niche, which had been defined through a regulatory monopoly.

In the past, thrifts had a built-in, regulated advantage on both the asset and the liability side. On the asset side, thrifts were the only providers of long-term home owner financing. That was the purpose for which they were created. They were the fuel behind the housing industry. Their role as the sole mortgage lender, however, has effectively been displaced in the past decade by mortgage bankers and commercial banks, both of which operate on high volumes. These volumes create economies of scale against which many thrifts cannot effectively compete. This, coupled with the advent of a national deposit market and the elimination of the quarter percent rate differential on savings which thrifts used to have by law, wreaked havoc in both the asset and liability sides of the thrifts' balance sheets. Their traditional position as the recipient of long-term savings and the provider of long-term housing finance has been eroded.

The thrift's traditional position in the marketplace has indeed been eliminated, yet many strong thrifts exist which have the capacity to survive. The purpose of this book is to discuss the strategic alternatives available to the survivors which build on their competitive advantages and strengths, while expanding their stategic focus beyond the traditional residential real estate lending. This past focus, although a viable position for some, can no longer support the whole industry. Some survivors should, therefore, consider the strategic alternatives available to them, and select those which best capitalize upon their market position, financial condition, other resources, and customer relationships. This book outlines some of those strategic alternatives, and also provides tools which thrifts can use to identify the future success paths which suit them best.

I

The Dead and the Wounded

The thrift industry has shrunk in half from the mid-1980s to 1992. Of the over 4,000 thrifts that were alive in 1985, both savings and loans and savings banks, only approximately 2,300 institutions are around today. Many question the viability of these survivors even now. This uncertainty is to be expected given the number of insitutions that are not in capital compliance with regulatroy requirements and the increasing demand for immediate compliance by the regulators. The industry has suffered mass death and has been continuously hemorrhaging since the mid-1980s.

   This section briefly describes the events which brought about the drastic shrinkage of the industry and the contribution of the regulators to the thrifts' demise. Further, it evaluates the likelihood of survival of the business, and attempts to answer the question, "Is there a healthy core that will survive and even prosper in the future?"

1

The Sins of the Past: With Regulations Like These, Who Needs Enemies?

The thrift industry has been regulated by an extensive and elaborate structure which affected almost every aspect of business conduct. There are several reasons why the regulatory environment that thrifts operate in has developed in the way it has. Rightly or wrongly, the primary motivation for the development of regulation has been to serve a public interest role. Initially, regulation was advocated to promote safety, soundness, and economic stability. Additionally, regulation was intended to facilitate housing finance through the creation of tax and interest rate advantages that protected thrifts from competition. To a degree, regulation was also seen as a way to enhance the government's revenue-generating capabilities through imposition of various fees. However, ultimately, the regulatory framework of the thrift industry was designed to enhance the safety and soundness of the depository system.

Regardless of the motivation for the development of regulations, no one disputes the fact that, to a large extent, the thrift industry owes its early existence to the legislative walls that had partitioned the United States financial system into separate commercial banking, savings and mortgage lending, insurance, investment banking, and non-financial segments. The legal and market conditions have changed dramatically since the creation and imposition of early regulations such as Regulation Q, which ensured a rate advantage provided to the thrifts by law. Following the lead of changes in the marketplace, the legislative walls separating these various segments in the financial system have crumbled. The legislative framework slowly followed market-driven changes. The geographic restraints imposed by the McFadden and Douglas Acts have been, and probably will continue to be, weakened. The rate-related restraints that afforded thrifts a ready source of funds were removed with the phaseout of Regulation Q. The phase out, in turn, was prompted by the introduction of the money market funds, which permitted, for the first time, disintermediation of depository accounts. The phaseout of Regulation Q and the introduction of money market accounts offered by depository and non-depository institutions alike eliminated the ready, low-cost sources of funds which thrifts have enjoyed in the past.

Regulatory Reform: The Response to the Elimination of the Thrifts' Monopoly

The product and legal advantages that erected barriers to competitive entry around the thrifts were designed to preserve the safety and soundness of the industry. Instead, they often promoted an isolationist mentality and management style that was not sharpened by healthy competition. As these barriers were removed, thrifts had to learn to compete. In addition, rising interest rates created serious deposit disintermediation and interest rate problems in the thrift industry. The 1980 Depository Institutions Deregulation and Monetary Control Act and the 1982 Garn-St Germain Act were enacted to address, among other issues, the problems mentioned above. The first piece of legislation brought about the phasing out of Regulation Q and eliminated the competitive advantage that thrifts had on the liability side of the balance sheet. The second piece of legislation was intended to deregulate the asset side and broaden thrift powers. It permitted adjustable rate mortgages, and other loans and investments beyond the home loans. In theory, the idea was to permit savings associations to earn more money so they could afford to pay competitive rates for deposits and also build their net worth back up to minimum requirements. Together, these two pieces of legislation constituted the largest part of the initial industry deregulation.

The Thrifts' Response to Expanded Powers

Despite this deregulation initiative during the late 1970s and early 1980s, rapidly rising rates, coupled with unprecedented rate volatility (Figure 1–1), exposed the thrifts to significant interest rate risk which was followed by heavy losses. Their fixed-rate mortgages continued to yield a fixed-rate return, while the cost of deposits and CDs used to fund the mortgages skyrocketed, thereby creating a negative margin for many institutions. Paying more for the deposits than what the assets earned could not be made up by volume. It indicated a structural flaw, a level of interest rate risk embedded within the thrifts' portfolios which they could not outgrow. Further, imprudent expansion into new lines of business such as commercial loans and real estate equity participations, both of which were encouraged by the deregulation, caused a number of thrifts to become insolvent.

Figure 1–1: Prime Rate (Number of Changes per Year from 1970–1991)

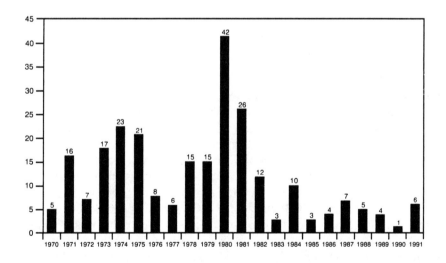

The existing Federal Home Loan Bank Board Forbearance Policy, which permitted undercapitalized thrifts to remain open, in combination with the thrifts' broader asset powers and the security of insured deposits, provided both the incentives and the opportunities for many thrifts to behave imprudently. Additionally, other thrifts used the expanded powers they received during the 1980s to move into new businesses that exposed them to more credit risks than traditional home mortgage lending. They expanded into commercial lending and other types of unsecured lending which, by definition, created more risk than secured residential estate lending (if properly done). Further, thrifts delved into real estate ventures, assuming that their knowledge of the residential lending market would be leveraged through these activities. They did not realize that real estate acquisition, development and construction loans are highly specialized, highly risky businesses.

By the mid–1980s, more than 750 thrifts were, in fact, insolvent or poorly capitalized, and the industry's insurance fund was bankrupt. As a response to this crisis, Congress passed the Financial Institutions Regulatory Reform Act (FIRREA) in August 1989. The law set stricter rules for levels of capitalization, encouraged reconcentration on mortgage investments, prohibited certain types of risky investments, and required higher fees for examination, supervision, and insurance. In return for complying with the requirements of FIRREA, thrifts were allowed continued access to Federal Home Loan Bank advances and to receive the benefits of favorable tax treatment with respect to bad debt deductions.

Regulatory Overreaction to the Thrifts' Problems: FIRREA

FIRREA was another example of a piece of legislation that intended to heal but pushed many more institutions beyond the brink of survival. FIRREA did not provide the industry with the necessary transition time in order to accomplish the changes it required. Instead, instant compliance was expected. As a result, healthy institutions became insolvent overnight. In addition, many healthy real estate developers and builders who obtained financing from savings and loan associations and savings banks were put out of business overnight with the instant imposition of loans to one borrower (LTOB) limitations. LTOB prevented thrifts from extending credit to major borrowers beyond 15 percent of their net worth, instantly reducing available credit from 100 percent of net worth. The result: healthy projects ran out of funding immediately exacerbating the real estate crisis nationwide. FIRREA with all its good intentions, brought about at least as much damage as benefit.

The regulators recognized that, while FIRREA went a long way toward dealing with emergency needs for capital and regulatory reform, it is insufficient to set the parameters for a healthy industry. In fact, many observers were concerned that FIRREA symbolizes the government's determination to eliminate the thrift industry altogether. As a result, seven pieces of legislation were under examination by Congress in the 1991/92 session to further restructure the industry. All proposals are intended to further heal the ailing thrifts and separate the wounded and dying from the healthy core. The impact of these proposals, as well as FIRREA, has been to impose upon the thrift industry the discipline already present in the commercial banking industry and other segments of the depository institutions. Only core earnings and tangible assets were ultimately to be considered. A full analysis of the risks imbedded in each institution's portfolio—credit risk, interest rate risk, liquidity risk, and the like—was required.

Seeking a Strategic Identity

These regulatory and legislative changes are creating a new and interesting dilemma for all members of the thrift industry, successful and unprofitable alike. In the past, the industry had a clear strategic position. It was created post depression in order to fuel individual home ownership in the United States. Its goal was long term home financing. Discrete sources of funds were designed to fund this financing activity. With the elimination of the thrifts' monopoly on either activity, the question many thrift executives pose to themselves is: "What is the raison d'etre of their institution?" Is financing home building in America still a viable strategic niche for the business, or should thrifts seek alternative strategic positions for future survival and prosperity?

The purpose of this book is to examine this key question and offer some solutions to the dilemma facing thrifts today; should we stick to our knitting or should we venture anew? Doing what thrifts have done best in the past is an appealing strategic alternative. Thrifts know the real estate business very well. Many thrifts have been consistently profitable throughout the industry debacle by doing what they traditionally have done best, generating long-term loans and funding them with relatively inexpensive stable deposits. These profitable thrifts are all over the country and they may feel that doing what they have done all along will continue to serve them in the future.

Further, diversification into other areas of business has been tried by many in the early 1980s following deregulation and has proven disastrous. Many new lines of business which appeared attractive became the downfall of hundreds of thrifts around the country due to lack of expertise, economic downturn, and other factors. Therefore, many thrift executives feel that going back to basics and sticking to their roots is the best strategic alternative.

By the same token, major, often more economical, alternatives to thrifts as providers of home financing have emerged. These range from government-sponsored agencies, such as Fannie Mae and Freddie Mac, to mega mortgage bankers such as Citibank, Great Western, and Fleet. These organizations can capitalize upon unparalleled economies of scale in offering home financing. They are gradually taking over the market to the extent that today the commercial banking share of the home mortgage business is greater than that of the thrifts for the first time in history. These trends and others indicate that "doing what we've always done best" may not be a viable solution to many institutions. How does a savings and loan institution make the determination of what is the most likely future course to success, and which of the alternative paths are right for their particular institution?

2

Is There a Healthy Core?

The traditional role of thrift institutions has been to provide its customers the three components of home mortgage lending: 1) loan origination, 2) loan holding credit provision (bearing credit and liquidity risk) and 3) loan servicing. In the past, due to the regulatory environment and the absence of secondary markets, these three functions were almost always served by the same institution for any given loan. As the industry became deregulated, Fannie Mae and Freddie Mac were introduced, and competition for funds increased, interest rates rose and secondary markets developed. The resulting, intensifying competition has driven many thrifts into insolvency. Among the successful survivors, some industry observers see an increasing trend towards diversification and strategic specialization. These strategic specializations are identified by the Government Accounting Office as shown in Table 2–1.

Diversification: Expansion of the Thrifts' Business Focus

This continuing trend away from the traditional and toward specialization and diversification will create niche opportunities for thrifts able to capitalize on

Table 2–1: Strategic Specializations

Business Strategy	1979	1982	1985	1989
Traditional	98.8%	83.7%	48.7%	38.9%
Commercial	0.3	0.8	7.4	5.7
Mortgage Banking	1.1	1.9	3.6	7.4
Security Investment	0.4	1.3	6.2	13.4
Real Estate Development	0.0	0.1	3.2	1.6
Eclectic/Diversified	0.7	14.6	34.0	36.2

Type	Criteria
Traditional	Permanent residential mortgages are at least 60% of assets
Commercial	The sum of consumer loans and commercial or non-residential loans is at least 30% of assets
Mortgage Banking	Loans serviced for others are at least 70%
Security/Equity Investment	Investment in service corporations plus investment securities are 45% of assets
Real Estate Development	Real estate held for development plus construction loans and land loans are 30% of assets
Eclectic	Thrifts that do not meet these criteria

Source: GAO

strengths and opportunities they already have or are able to acquire. Examples include:

1. *Consumer Finance Company.* Thrifts still have, and are expected to have, a fairly low cost of funds. They have a loyal customer base which provides low-cost savings which are typically stable and reliable. Only major shifts in the yield curve, like on the late 1970s and early 1980s, will bring about another major wave of disintermediation. These relationships with the consumer can be parlayed into an effective consumer lending operation, using products ranging from credit cards and home equity loans to executive loans, auto loans, and unsecured personal loans. That is a natural evolution for a thrift with a strong retail base and solid experience

of certain types of consumer lending. Thus, thrifts may displace some consumer finance companies in their quest to find their own new strategic identity.

2. *Real Estate Finance Company.* Some institutions have been successful in "going back to basics." They maintain their niche in mortgage lending and have done so profitably through the years. Despite fluctuations in the real estate market, they have demonstrated strong performance and minimal loan losses. These institutions will continue to occupy that niche as real estate financing companies, providing both variable and fixed-rate mortgages to customers.

A variation on that theme is the secondary market institution. Those thrifts that have developed a successful origination network as well as a strong servicing capability have been able to build a fee income base in addition to the margin-based business. The secondary market niche is a natural extension of the real estate lending business, where thrifts have traditionally had expertise and strong market presence. It capitalizes upon their market identity and customer recognition as well as using excess servicing capacity in a volume sensitive business. Many thrifts have been relying on their ability to securitize mortgages and focus on origination and servicing only, as is demonstrated in Table 2–2.

I believe the prospects for institutions that can take advantage of the continued growth and importance of the secondary markets are quite good. While building the necessary origination network and servicing capability may be difficult, those institutions that can pass these hurdles will be afforded significant growth opportunities while capitalizing upon long-standing strategic strengths.

3. *Community Banking Company.* Most surviving thrifts already consider themselves community banks. Their specific charter is immaterial, almost an obsolete relic. Many successful thrifts recognize that their survival depends on their ability to effectively compete with other community banks in providing a full range of services to consumers and small businesses in their community. The key to success here is a combination of high-quality service and an appropriate product line which more fully meets customer needs.

A successful conversion into a community bank will require many thrifts to supplement their thrift skills with commercial banking skills. Some have already done so, as indicated in Table 2–1 by the growth of the "Eclectic" or diversified category. Also, there are more commercial banking executives who have become thrift executives today than ever before. This trend must continue in order to bring about a successful transition to community banking. In implementing this strategy, thrifts will build upon their customer loyalty and strong community presence to more fully meet customers' needs with non-real estate consumer loans, non-CD

11

Table 2–2: Share of Total Residential Mortgage Debt Directly Held by Lender

Year	Total	Thrifts	Banks	Life Insurance	Federal Agency	Mort. Pools	Other
1970	$ 338.2	55.8%	13.5%	12.6%	7.4%	0.1%	10.6%
1975	591.4	53.0	14.0	6.3	8.5	5.0	13.3
1980	1,124.1	48.2	15.4	3.3	6.8	11.6	14.7
1985	1,702.5	37.8	13.9	1.9	7.2	24.7	14.5
1989	2,690.7	29.2	14.7	1.5	6.3	34.6	13.7

investments (such as mutual funds), and other products and services. For these institutions especially, quality service will be paramount. The factors that affect the quality of service delivery—such as technology, training, and responsiveness—will be a major implementation focus.

Industry Size

The research department of the former U.S. League of Savings Institutions, now Savings and Community Bankers Association has produced excellent information and projections on this topic.

According to League research, during the past two years, the thrift business has experienced significant shrinkage. Over 600 institutions, representing 20 percent of the industry, have disappeared or have been placed in the Resolution Trust Corporation (RTC) for resolution. At the same time, the total assets of the business have plummeted by $340 billion, or 23 percent.

Even after this sharp contraction, the process is still far from complete. According to the Office of Thrift Supervision (OTS), there are another 218 thrifts having $151 billion of assets that are scheduled for resolution by the RTC. Further, the current recession and the losses experienced by institutions with marginal capital positions clearly suggest that the number of firms destined for the RTC is bound to increase substantially over the next 12 months.

Given these observations, it is clear that the thrift business has not only been shrinking rapidly but will continue to do so. This situation raises a number of fundamental questions about the future of the thrift business.

Why is the thrift industry shrinking so significantly? How much more will the business shrink over the relatively near term? Will most of today's thrifts simply disappear or is there a healthy core of survivors?

Of course, the answers to these questions will provide insight into an even more basic issue: Will there be a core of healthy thrift institutions that could support a separate, identifiable thrift business?

Why Is the Thrift Business Shrinking?

As many thrifts have been closed or placed in the RTC, people formed the impression that the thrift industry is in a state of collapse. Poor earnings reported by a number of large companies at the end of 1990, the serious problems evident in the real estate sector, and the troubles of the RTC have reinforced this impression.

In fact, most of the thrifts now being closed are not recent failures. Instead, they are institutions that failed long ago and are just now being resolved. In this regard, some history is instructive.

At the end of 1979 the nation's savings institutions consisted of 4,038 firms having $567 billion of assets. These companies had real tangible capital of $31.5 billion for a tangible capital-to-assets ratio of 5.56 percent. By the end of 1982, there were 751 fewer thrift institutions. The regulatory capital of the business fell $6.3 billion while GAAP capital plunged $11.3 billion. This lowered the regulatory capital ratio of the business to 3.69 percent and the Generally Accepted Accounting Principles (GAAP) capital ratio to 2.96 percent. More important is the reduction of the industry's tangible capital. By the end of 1982, the tangible capital of the business had fallen $27.7 billion, to $3.8 billion. The tangible capital ratio of the business was an incredibly low 0.55 percent.

At that time, public policy was such that neither the industry nor the regulators would not recognize this reality. Regulators and others did not focus on tangible capital. Instead, the problems of the business were viewed in the context of regulatory capital. Contributing to the potential for problems, the business was allowed to grow. As its tangible capital disappeared, the total assets of the business increased $120 billion or 21 percent.

Table 2–3 shows the tangible insolvent firms in the business since the end of 1982. At the end of that year, there were 317 tangible insolvent firms operating with roughly $200 billion of assets.

This number peaked at 690 tangible insolvents at year's end 1985. These firms had assets of $352 billion and a negative real capital totaling $17 billion.

Table 2–3: Tangible Insolvent Firms

Year-end	Number	Assets ($ Bill)	Tangible Capital ($ Bill)	Tangible Capital to Assets
1982	317	$199.6	($11.9)	-5.96%
1983	445	$263.4	($13.1)	-4.97%
1984	680	$355.1	($16.1)	-4.53%
1985	690	$351.6	($17.0)	-4.84%
1986	661	$336.6	($19.1)	-5.67%
1987	677	$360.8	($29.2)	-8.09%
1988	523	$302.7	($20.9)	-6.90%
1989	543	$312.7	($34.8)	-11.13%
June 1990	380	$214.6	($27.0)	-12.58%

Why were these institutions allowed to stay open? Because the standards at that time were set in terms of regulatory capital. As a result, only the worst were closed, while the others were allowed to grow in assets and in losses.

The first real reduction in the number of tangible insolvent institutions took place in 1988, due to intervention by the Federal Home Loan Bank Board (FHLBB.) Another big reduction took place during the first half of 1990, as the RTC actually began to operate. In fact, of the 380 tangible insolvent firms existing in June 1990, our data show 247 being operated by the RTC. Thus, the number of tangible insolvent thrifts operating as private firms had fallen to 137 institutions by mid-1990. In retrospect, it is clear that these failed firms should have been closed much earlier. Leaving them to operate turned out to be a disaster for the business and the taxpayer. This mistake was corrected in FIRREA.

When the decision was made to shift to a real tangible capital solvency standard, the fallout of the prior couple of years was mandated. Firms that had been insolvent on a tangible capital basis were recognized as having failed and in need of resolution. No one should be surprised that hundreds of savings institutions were closed. In other words, the thrift industry has been shrinking rapidly largely as a result of past failures and the delay in their closure, not in response to significant new failures.

What the FIRREA tangible capital standard did was recognize economic reality. It established a new basis upon which to define the healthy core of the business. The failure of these firms, therefore, should not be seen as evidence that the remaining thrift business is not viable. Nor does it imply that the business is getting weaker.

Are There Survivors?

Recent history shows that any effort to project who the thrift survivors will be involves a lot of guesswork. Still, existing data does provide some reasonable insights. The OTS classifications may be used to determine the number of viable institutions. According the the Office of Thrift Supervision, as of September 30, 1990 there were 2,389 private sector thrifts (i.e., excluding those under the control of the Resolution Trust Corporation), with total assets of $1,043.2 billion, or 22.7 percent below the year-end 1988 peak.

Of these private sector thrifts, 218 with assets of $151.0 billion are classified as Group 4 institutions. By the OTS's criteria, these institutions are destined for transfer to the RTC. Hence, they can be subtracted from the total figures for future projections.

There are another 356 institutions with assets of $191.3 billion in OTS's Group 3. These are institutions that fail to meet their current capital requirements (3 percent core, 1.5 percent tangible and 6.4 percent risk-based capital) and have been suffering consistent losses. Their chance of survival is highly suspect.

Excluding Groups 3 and 4 from the private sector thrift universe leaves 1,815 institutions with assets of $700.9 billion and deposits of $539.6 billion. These are the sum totals for the OTS's Groups 1 and 2.

Based on what we know about the OTS's group classification criteria, Groups 1 and 2 institutions are very likely survivors. Group 1 institutions meet all capital requirements and have been consistently profitable on an operating basis and on a net income basis. They also must have a high Management, Assets (quality) Capital, Risk Organization (MACRO) rating. Group 2 institutions have very similar characteristics, except they may have suffered a loss on one of the income measures, or they may have capital ratios not quite up to requirements, but they have the earnings potential to meet all requirements in the very near term. In addition to these numerical measures, the OTS may downgrade, but not upgrade, institutions based on the opinions of field examiners.

One difficulty with the OTS scheme is that it cannot be replicated by parties outside the OTS. This prevents a critical analysis of these institutions, since the only data available on these groups are what the OTS puts out in its press releases. Of course, there are other measures of survivability. For example, consider the set of institutions with 3 percent or more tangible capital. The reason 3 percent is the cutoff is that that 3 percent is the required level of tangible capital at the end of the phase-in period to higher capital standards. Using this criteria to identify healthy institutions, the result is not that much different from the OTS's Groups 1 and 2. As of September 30, 1990, there were 1,959 institutions with $642.9 billion in assets and $499.8 billion in deposits that had 3 percent or more tangible capital. They had an average tangible capital-to-asset ratio of 5.7 percent.

Another possibility is to look at those institutions meeting the 8 percent risk-based capital requirement. That, again, is the fully phased-in requirement. The justification for looking at this measure of capital is that in the Treasury's proposal for deposit insurance reform, risk-based capital plays a central role. Further, risk-based capital is becoming an increasingly important tool to create financial soundness. Using risk-based capital as the basis, the core business would consist of 1,726 institutions with total assets of $575.9 billion and total deposits of $443.3 billion.

A fourth and most stringent possible survivability test would be to combine the 3 percent tangible capital and the 8 percent risk-based capital requirements. In that case, the surviving industry totals 1,687 institutions, $538.0 billion in assets, and $418.2 in deposits.

Table 2–4 summarizes these four approaches to estimating the healthy core of the thrift business. Taken as a whole, they suggest that the core will include approximately 1,700 institutions having assets of roughly $500 billion. This would imply that the thrift business could stabilize at about one-half of its peak size, which was reached at the end of 1988.

Assuming that these estimates provide us with a reasonable guess, what does the thrift business of the future look like? For that purpose, consider the set of institutions with more than 3 percent tangible capital as a proxy for the future thrift industry. Their asset and deposit totals are very near the average for the four possibilities presented.

These institutions have a very low-risk profile. Their ratio of risk-weighted assets to total assets is only 57.6 percent. Along with their high capital, this low-risk portfolio results in a very high average risk-based capital ratio of 11.6 percent.

Over 54 percent of their assets are held in whole residential mortgage loans. Another 12.5 percent is in the form of mortgage-backed securities. Their cash and investments, i.e., liquid assets, total 12.8 percent of total assets.

Through the first nine months of 1990, these institutions earned $2.1 billion on an after-tax basis. They reported an annualized return on assets of 0.44 percent and an annualized return on equity of 6.84 percent. They had a healthy net interest margin equal to 2.28 percent. Although hardly impressive, these figures do indicate

Table 2–4: Thrift Industry Assets and Deposits by Institutional Capitalization Levels

	Number	Assets	Deposits
Groups 1 & 2	1,815	$ 700.9	$ 539.9
Tangible Capital Over 3%	1,959	$ 642.9	$ 499.5
Risk-based Capital Over 8%	1,736	$ 575.9	$ 443.3
Tangible Capital Over 3% &			
Risk-based Over 8%	1,687	$ 538.0	$ 418.2
Average	1,797	$ 614.4	$ 475.2
Year-end 1988	2,949	$1,348.9	$ 971.7
Absolute Change	(1,152)	$ (734.5)	$(496.6)
Percent Change	-39.1%	-54.4%	-51.1%

a core which by necessity (due to the stringent qualified lender test imposed on thrifts) is focused on real estate finance.

Table 2–5 presents some basic demographic data on these institutions. By number, the majority are mutuals, but these institutions represent only 27.5 percent of all assets. Institutions with federal charters are in the majority, both in terms of numbers and assets.

Over three-fourths of the institutions have less than $250 million in assets, but almost 58 percent of the assets are held by the 96 institutions (4.9 percent of the total) with more than $1 billion in assets. It is also worth noting that an institution with more than 3 percent tangible capital can be found in all 50 states, the District of Columbia, Guam, Puerto Rico and the Virgin Islands.

In summary, there is a healthy core of thrifts having roughly $500 billion of assets and a nationwide presence. What will be the strategic focus of the thrifts in the future? Will real estate continue to be the basis of commonality, or will other strategic alternatives arise? These questions are of particular relevance today since such strategic focus is a critical factor to the success of any financial institution.

Table 2–5: Thrift Industry Capitalization Profile

Capitalization by Charter	Number	Assets	Tangible Capital	Tangible Capital-Asset Ratio
Mutual institutions	1,143	$176.5	$ 12.3	7.0%
Percent of total	58.3%	27.5%	33.4%	NA
Stock institutions	816	$466.4	$ 24.5	5.3%
Percent of total	41.7%	72.5%	66.6%	NA
Federal charter	1,177	$514.7	$ 28.5	5.5%
Percent of total	60.1%	80.1%	77.4%	NA
State charter	782	$128.2%	$ 8.3	6.5%
Percent of total	39.9%	19.9%	22.6%	NA

Asset Size Distribution	Number	Percent of Total	Assets	Percent of Total
Under $100 million	1,051	53.6%	$ 51.0	7.9%
$100 - $250 million	496	25.3%	$ 77.9	12.1%
$250 - $500 million	213	10.9%	$ 73.3	11.4%
$500 - $1,000 million	103	5.3%	$ 70.6	11.0%
Over $1,000 million	96	4.9%	$370.1	57.6%
Total	1, 959	100.0%	$642.9	100.0%

Capitalization by Asset	Tangible Capital	Percent of Total	Tangible Capital-Asset Ratio
Under $100 million	$ 3.9	10.6%	7.6%
$100 - $250 million	$ 5.4	14.7%	6.9%
$250 - $500 million	$ 4.9	13.3%	6.7%
$500 - $1,000 million	$ 4.1	11.1%	5.8%
Over $1,000 million	$18.5	50.3%	5.0%
Total	$36.8	100.0%	5.7%

3

The Real Estate Focus: Is the Thrift's Role Obsolete? Lessons from Home and Around the World

The traditional real estate focus, primarily on residential real estate, may not be a defensible strategic niche for many thrifts in the future. As commercial banks and mortgage bankers overtake thrifts as the largest mortgage originators in the United States, a process which started long ago and continues today, the following question should be asked:

Are charter specialized mortgage lenders a relic of the past, or is home lending a viable future niche?

Is the Role of Specialized Home Lenders Obsolete?

It appears that charter specialization has become less important in the financial systems of many countries around the world. In many countries, specialized thrift and home financing institutions have been granted broader powers by legislative bodies, both on the asset and liability side of their balance sheets. As a result, those thrifts tended to become more like full-service banks and abandoned the charter-oriented focus. In most instances, the broader powers have been in the consumer financial services area, including services such as consumer checking, small consumer loans, insurance, some authority to finance commercial real estate, small commercial loans, etc.

A look at the course of development in the past ten years in the United States, Great Britian, South Africa, Australia, New Zealand, and Canada would lead one to conclude that charter specialized financial institutions have little future, that the specific-purpose deposit-taking financial institutions, such as the building societies and savings and loan associations that we knew 15 or 20 years ago, will become full service financial institutions. It seems that the thrift system that was so prominent in these countries will, in the near future, completely disappear into the various countries' depository financial institutions system. While it may retain its functional focus, it will lose its charter-based separate existence.

This development is not entirely the result of deregulation. Deregulation, of course, has made it *possible* for these institutions to become less and less charter specialized. In some cases, including in the United States, this development often merely recognized market realities. Either way, deregulation is not the *primary reason* for the change toward full service consumer banks.

The Changing Dynamics of the Depository Institutions' Marketplace

In the United States, deregulation followed as a result of the development of certain serious problems in our savings and loan system. It came with the passage of two pieces of legislation by the Congress: The Depository Institutions Deregulation and Monetary Control Act of 1980, and the Garn-St Germain Act of 1982. The first Act, passed in 1980, essentially began the dismantling of Regulation Q, a system put in place in 1933 wherein the Federal Government set maximum rates of interest that different categories of depository financial institutions could pay on deposits. The system of setting interest rate ceilings became very difficult to administer in the late 1970s, with rapidly rising interest rates and the resultant development of a whole new set of deposit-taking institutions known as money market funds—mutual funds with the assets invested wholly in short-term money market instruments, primarily government securities.

With the inflation we had beginning in the late 1970s and the resulting high interest rates in the short-term market, the money market funds flourished. They had a product which offered liquidity similar to savings accounts yet were able to pay significantly higher rates of interest than banks and savings and loan associations could pay under the Regulation Q ceilings. Savings and loan associations could not afford to pay these rates even if permissible, given their asset portfolios of long-term, fixed-rate mortgages written when interest rates were much lower.

Lifting the Regulation Q limitations was perceived as a way to fix this problem. Regulation Q ceilings were to be phased out by gradually raising rates paid on deposits. The deposit side of the business was thus becoming "deregulated." Banks and savings and loan associations were being allowed to compete with the money market funds and the higher interest rate short-term investments available in the market.

To hold on to their savings, however, savings and loan associations found themselves having to pay more for their deposits than they were accustomed to, or, for that matter, than they were earning. The business ran deeply in the red in the late 1970s and early 1980s and lost most of its net worth. The legislative solution to this problem was more deregulation—this time on the asset side of the balance sheet. New legislation permitted adjustable interest rate mortgages—and also permitted, and strongly encouraged, loans and investments other than home loans.

In theory, the idea was to permit associations to earn more money so they could afford to pay competitive rates for money and halt the diversification process, while building their net worth back up to minimum requirements. Further, diversification out of the real estate business was perceived to be a risk reduction, profit enhancement tool. Deregulation also permitted a new type of owner-manager to come into the business (through the creation of a service corporation entity), whereby thrifts could fund real estate projects as well as participate in their success through equity ownership.

None of the moves toward deregulation worked out as intended, and some had disastrous results. Fewer than half of the institutions in existence in 1980 will live as savings and loan associations into 1992 or 1993. The question is: what will *their* future be?

The Commoditization of Thrifts' Assets and Liabilities in the United States

There were several other conditions, most of which are unique to the United States, that led to the unhappy record of our institutions in the 1980s. Until 1981 thrifts could not make adjustable rate mortgages. Most other countries have had them for decades, making their institutions better able to deal with the problems posed by inflation-induced, high short-term interest rates. Even where adjustable rate mortgages became permissible, they often could not compete with the market-place—most borrowers prefer a fixed-rate mortgage.

Further, as a result of the advent of high-speed computers and instantaneous electronic systems of communication as well as the presence of Fannie Mae and Freddie Mac, the mortgage market has been semi-nationalized and has changed markedly. We have seen an enormous expansion in the operations of two federal agencies operating in the secondary mortgage market—the Federal National Mortgage Association (Fannie Mae) and the Federal Home Loan Mortgage Corporation (Freddie Mac). Most home mortgages made today are those eligible for sale to one of these agencies. In fact, most mortgages made today—including most of those made by savings and loan associations—are sold to these agencies.

There they are securitized, that is, they are packaged and used as collateral for mortgage-backed bonds. These mortgage-backed bonds are purchased by bond funds, life insurance companies, pension funds, banks, individuals and, yes, savings and loan associations and savings banks. These federal companies are privately owned, but they are, for all practical purposes, agencies of the federal government. They are financial intermediaries channeling family savings and other long-term funds into the residential mortgage market, a function once almost exclusively performed by savings and loan associations. The unique role which the thrifts once played in financing home purchases in America has been displaced by a nationwide institutional market which created liquidity and economies of scale with which no single thrift could effectively compete. The once local asset origination mode of the mortgage market has been replaced by a national mortgage market, which enabled any originator to sell the asset almost instantaneously.

At the same time, technology has also made possible the operation of nation-wide CD markets, money market, and bond funds. The money market and bond funds offered formidable competition to the deposit function of savings and loans institutions. The liability side, once a monopoly ensured by Regulation Q, has also evolved into a commodity-like national deposit market, including deposit brokers and mutual funds. This competition for the once protected deposits was now taking place while Freddie Mac and Fannie Mae became overwhelming competitors on the loan side through the securitization of residential mortgages. In the United States today the savings and loan business is no longer relied upon as a major source of funds for home buying and home building.

Several reasons existed in the past for the specialized nature of the savings and loan associations in the United States. Like institutions in other countries, thrifts were created to finance home ownership and were dedicated to that purpose. The law and their charter kept them essentially confined to home lending. Income tax laws were written to provide the business with protection against the earnings pressures that come from open competitive markets. The protection against competitive pressures was provided in the United States essentially through Regulation Q. It gave savings and loan associations a competitive advantage of one-quarter percent over the maximum interest rate which commercial banks were permitted to pay for savings deposits, and it prevented other associations from paying a predatory rate of interest.

Savings and loan associations were prevented from competing too vigorously with one another in many other ways. For example, branches were limited, allowable market areas carefully drawn, and new entrants into the business limited. These measures essentially guaranteed a steady supply of deposits into the thrifts, as well as ensured their prominence as mortgage originators in their territory. Competition was restricted not only relative to other institutions but also with respect to other thrifts. The result was assured profitability.

About the same time as Congress changed the basic savings and loan law in 1982 to broaden lending and investment opportunities, Congress also changed the income tax law to lessen the tax incentive to specialize in the home mortgage business. At the same time, other parts of the financial system were being deregulated. Commercial banks have been expanding their services to fields once served almost exclusively by thrift institutions. Citibank, for example, is now the largest mortgage lender in the United States. Overall, banks are outstripping thrifts in mortgage origination. This mirrors developments in other countries. Arrangements to limit competition between building societies, such as the system of recommended rates in Great Britian, began to disappear at about the same time as Regulation Q began its final phaseout in the United States. The financial services marketplace in most countries is now an open market, laissez-faire system.

Strategic Options to Deal with Eroding Profitability

Profitability continues to elude some of the remaining thrift institutions. It is hard to be profitable when staying exclusively in the traditional home mortgage business, now a highly commoditized market, although some are quite successful at it. At the same time, the thrift industry's record of successful diversification into other lending and investment opportunities is poor, to say the least. The profitable institutions are those that have become extremely efficient in originating (i.e., making), selling, and servicing home loans. There is great economy of scale in the home mortgage business. As a result, the most profitable home mortgage lenders tend to be the large savings and loan associations, large commercial banks, and national mortgage bankers whose business consists wholly of making loans for sale, primarily to Freddie Mac and Fannie Mae. These mortgage banks, which do not depend on the savings of the public for funding, have all kinds of cost-effective advantages over the institutions that take in savings and small investment accounts from the public and invest those savings in home mortgage loans.

Other profitable savings and loan-type institutions in the United States are those that serve well-defined markets, and do an excellent job in serving those markets. They also tend to be well capitalized. The large, nationwide, efficient lenders and those servicing a small niche in the market will survive and prosper as specialized mortgage lending institutions.

Other savings institutions will prefer to go the way of multi-purpose institutions which the law now clearly permits. They can either plan for their acquisition or adopt a specific business focus, often gradually taking on the characteristics of a commercial bank. Already, most savings and loan associations today are known as banks or savings banks, even though they operate under the savings and loan law and charter and remain almost exclusively home mortgage lenders. Further, the Federal Savings and Loan Insurance Corporation no longer exists. For 58 years it was an independent federal agency responsible for the savings and loan business and, with the U.S. League of Savings Institutions, acted to serve and protect the business and to maintain its special character. The deposits in thrift institutions are now insured by the Federal Deposit Insurance Corporation which also insures bank deposits, and they are examined and supervised by personnel in the Treasury Department, as are the commercial banks.

Deregulation does not mean the end of specialized home mortgage lending institutions in the United States, but rather the decline of the niche. It no longer will be able to support 3,000 companies as it did 20 years ago. The number of traditional mortgage lending specialized institutions (as distinguished form mortgage bankers) will decline. Many will convert community bank-like institutions into serving local markets.

Before deregulation, basic management and operating decisions of thrift institutions were made by the government. You were either in the building society business or in some other business. If you were in the building society business, you did only what the building society law said you could do. Today, in many countries, the nature of these institutions has changed. Management decisions and marketplace forces determine success, failure, and type of activity. What these institutions will do or become, whether by decision of management or market forces, will most likely depend on whichever course of action will be considered most profitable. Certainly the day when our business was considered a quasi-public service business, dedicated to promoting thrift and home ownership, is over, except possibly in the developing countries. The thrift business today is just another business. Profit opportunities will determine the nature of the business in the future.

4

The Wounded

The thrift industry has already shrunk in half. Of the 3,200 savings and loan associations that existed in 1985, only 1,900 are in existence today. Of those, 300 still do not meet the capital requirements imposed by FIRREA. Of these ailing thrifts, how many can turn themselves around and earn their way back to a healthy capital position?

Thrift Turnaround--A Difficult Proposition

Many obstacles stand in the way of nursing sick thrifts back to health. It is harder to achieve thrift turnarounds than in other industries. The first reason for this difficulty is that the thrifts have fewer options available to them then other industries. Strategies such as restructuring financially, selling business units, or modernizing, are not clearly available to thrifts while being used extensively in other industries.

1. *Financial restructuring.* Financial restructuring is not possible at this point. The capital markets do not trust the thrift industry. Only top performers can issue

investment-grade debt. It is extremely difficult to recapitalize in public or private offerings. Those thrifts that are capital starved as a result of the instantaneous conversion of goodwill capital into dust cannot replenish that capital from sources that are typically available to other industries. Instead, they are operating with a "black hole" of negative net worth, which makes it twice as hard to break even.

The most likely investors in such thrifts are corporate traders or other financial institutions that seek to acquire them "for a song." Bargain hunters abound, but their interest does not necessarily lie in turning the institution around. Many are looking at the thrifts as an inexpensive way to acquire additional deposits or a going concern and a business base. However, most of those do not perceive the thrifts as stand-alone entities which, following capital infusion, will nurse themselves back to health and thus improve the return to the shareholders through capital appreciation.

2. *Divesting Subsidiaries.* Divesting has enabled many institutions to turn themselves around. Many commercial banks are paring down through the sale of profitable credit card portfolios or mortgage servicing operations, thus permitting themselves to focus on the primary business and reinvesting the profits from the sale in those businesses. Most thrifts, however, own no gems which can be sold at hefty premiums.

If they do own such gems, including high yielding, high-quality fixed-rate mortgage portfolios or other attractive assets, these would be in all likelihood the assets which are making the highest profit. Selling those would cut the thrift's earning ability significantly, and in a way, bring about the demise of the institution despite realizing sale profits. Therefore, ailing thrifts which attempt to sell the pearls among their portfolio find themselves between a rock and a hard place. It is precisely those pearls that allow the thrifts to survive through a solid income stream and consistent performance. Selling those precious assets will incur profits but at the same time penalize the thrift's future, on occasion beyond the point of no return.

3. *Modernizing.* Modernizing the operations of the thrift often entails a large initial outlay for a computer system. The capital required to implement such a program would deplete capital in the short term to a significant extent. However, modernizing and improving operations through outsourcing is a viable alternative to ailing thrifts that are inefficient and antiquated from an operational perspective. This alternative may not solve the problems with thrifts with poor loan quality problems or with no capital but may impose their competitive posture for future growth.

4. *Inadequate capital.* This itself is a direct cause for S&L's low profitability. With less capital, the institution lacks some of the "free" funds on which it doesn't pay any interest, namely the capital. These cost-free funds earn the bank, at minimum, the Treasury rate, thereby contributing to profitability. *Standard & Poor's* conducted a study of thrift turnarounds. Candidates for this study, all publicly owned, were drawn from among the following:

◆ Substandard earning performers

◆ Those that had submitted the thrift capital plans to the Office of Thrift Supervision (OTS)

◆ Thrifts that had announced major restructurings

◆ S&Ls that had recently achieved capital compliance

Each candidate was evaluated for:

◆ Ability to enhance or resume core profitability

◆ The likelihood of hidden surprises that will surface, such as big additions to reserves

◆ Management capability

◆ Competitive advantages

The *Standard & Poor's* study concluded that most candidates were deeply insolvent, had serious asset quality problems, and were not remotely profitable on a core earnings basis. The study went so far as to state that, "it was challenging to find companies with odds of success as good as 1 in 10." The one success story has many of the characteristics recommended in this book to enable thrifts to retain, achieve, and maintain success. That particular thrift was formed in 1982 through the assisted supervisory mergers of thrifts in New York, Connecticut, and Massachusetts. It became a wholesale shop.

It invested in purchased mortgages, mortgage-backed securities, and junk bonds funded by Federal Home Loan Bank borrowings, brokered deposits, repurchase agreements, and other capital markets vehicles. In July of 1988, the company abandoned its wholesale focus and reverted to a traditional retail thrift. Two and half years later there is ample evidence that the strategy worked. The company returned to profitability for two consecutive quarters; it also met all three capital tests mandated by the bailout law. Capital compliance was obtained by downsizing the balance sheet, combined with reclassification of the company's two preferred stock issues to obligations of a newly formed holding company rather than the thrift unit. Profitability was restored through:

◆ Ceasing all non-thrift activities

◆ Reducing reliance on wholesale funding sources

◆ Emphasizing the origination of adjustable rate mortgages

◆ Branch consolidation

◆ Centralization of loan processing operations

◆ Simplification of product line.

The drop-in, short-term interest rates since September 1990 also greatly contributed to the healing of the company. Tangible capital thereby more than doubled within one year, as did the interest rate spread. Total assets were cut by half. General and administrative costs were cut to some extent, while fee income rose significantly. Although the company's interest rate spread is still well below its peers', it has already reached profitability on a core earnings basis.

Significant challenges remain in improving the spread and bringing the snow-balling, nonperforming assets which reflect the slump in northeast real estate to a halt. Large reserve additions are likely over the next several quarters. Nonetheless, this institution revised its strategic focus, and as a result improved its position significantly. There are lessons to be learned from this one, particularly as evidence of the performance implications of a clear strategic focus, the importance of managing the basics and leveraging existing strengths.

The Government's Role in Eliminating the Wounded

There are many practical problems facing ailing thrifts in bringing about their turnaround. In addition to the objective difficulties in the environment, which include intensifying competition, depleted capital, and the inability to replenish it; and the collapse of the real estate market and its effects on supply, demand, and profitability of the mortgage business, the government has made a major, and some say conscious contribution to the elimination of ailing thrifts. The environment itself made it difficult for those thrifts to turn themselves around. The government is mounting additional obstacles designed to prevent sick thrifts from healing themselves, and sometimes even pushing them over the brink. The following are examples of specific government acts which appear to be designed to eliminate the "wounded."

1. *Loan Classifications.* Extremely harsh loan classification examination decisions have become commonplace in the industry. Unsuspecting observers may conclude that the government has made a decision to eliminate those thrifts which are teetering on the brink through classification and reserve requirement decisions of loan portfolios. Specifically, there have been instances where a fully performing loan, current on both the principal and interest, has been classified as the value of the collateral deteriorated. This took place even though the collateral was a merely secondary payment source and the primary payment source has performed well. These non-performing loans are aggravating the problems of capital poor thrifts.

Many thrifts around the country are convinced that the government is out to put the industry out of business and that the classifications process is an easy tool to achieve that objective. When a loan is classified, existing capital evaporates and the profitability of the thrift is severely taxed. Since reserves must be accrued against each classified asset, the arbitrariness and "no appeal" nature of some recent loan classifications support the notion that the government is out to weed out the weaker institutions in the thrift industry, leaving only the very strongest.

2. *"By the Book" Examinations.* These examinations are another example of the government using the tools available to it to eliminate surviving thrifts. Many examinations are conducted with total disregard to special circumstances, which may explain the particular characteristics of the loan. For example, prior to the imposition of the new FIRREA loans to one borrower limitations, a healthy $1 billion thrift extended a loan to a major builder to build a hotel. The construction loan was then converted to a permanent commercial mortgage upon the successful completion of the project. The loan was current and performing.

However, examiners required the loan amount to be reduced to comply with the new loan to one borrower requirements. As a result, the builder went bankrupt, since additional financing was not available during the credit crunch of post FIRREA days when many credit extenders, both thrifts and commercials banks, realized that any real estate loan booked would be very likely to be reserved against in the next examination, thereby making it an unattractive loan. There are many other examples of "by the book" examinations which resulted in turning good loans into bad loans and turning healthy builders into an endangered species.

3. *Prevention of Thrift Conversion to Other Charters Through Regulations.* Many thrifts considered converting to other charters to be an ingredient in their plan to

turn themselves around. However, the bad debt recapture requirements and Qualified Lender Test (QTL) requirements are significant obstacles to overcome in such
conversion. As a result, very few thrifts with asset quality problems could afford to
convert to other charters. Similarly, QTL requirements limited the thrift's ability to
diversify beyond traditional "qualifying" loans. As a result, they remained unattractive as potential acquisition candidates to commercial banks and other acquirers
who shy away from real estate lending. Further, they could not diversify effectively
into other forms of profitable customer lending. The industry's continued efforts in
Washington to overturn these restrictions remain unsuccessful. The government's
well-intentioned regulations result in inhibiting the thrift's ability to improve their
condition.

4. *Mounting Obstacles on Capital Infusion Initiatives.* The thrift industry has
been seriously under-capitalized for many years. This became even more apparent
after FIRREA, the change in accounting for goodwill and the elimination of Generally Accepted Accounting Principles (GAAP) accounting. Ongoing efforts to recapitalize the industry have been slow and have met with only limited success. A
primary impediment to attracting capital to the industry was the uncertainty associated with it. Frequent regulatory changes and harsh examinations became commonplace, both of which have had a devastating impact on the balance sheet.
These, coupled with a slowing economy and a precarious real estate industry, have
been major deterrents to potential investors in bringing about the recapitalization of
the industry.

In reality, however, these external circumstances were not the only reasons
for recapitalization difficulties. In addition, the Office of Thrift Supervision has
created perhaps the single greatest hurdle to recapitalization of the industry: Thrift
Bulletin 5a. Thrift Bulletin 5a is an internal policy statement that requires a thrift to
meet its "fully phased in" FIRREA capital requirements upon completion of a
recapitalization or change of ownership. In the absence of meeting the "fully
phased in" requirement, i.e., 8 percent of risk-based assets less any non-qualifying
investments, the investors would be required to sign a capital maintenance agreement, which means that they will replenish depleted capital if future losses occur,
and that they have the demonstrated financial ability (e.g., provide an irrevocable
letter of credit) to meet any future capital calls. This internal policy is being rigidly
applied to all recapitalization or change of control applications, and has, in effect,
slammed the door on new capital for dozens of institutions.

Take this case for example: A $300 million mutual thrift has achieved profit-
able operations following a change in management. The thrift is below capital
requirements for all three ratios. A consortium of foreign institutional investors has

committed $100 million for investment in U.S. thrifts. Their objective: solid returns through capital gains after five to ten years. The group was prepared to inject $11 million worth of capital into the $300 million thrift through a modified stock conversion. The regulators have delayed approving the transaction for eighteen months, and have not approved it to date. The reason: the thrift still has a non-includable investment in real estate which was acquired prior to FIRREA.

The institution has successfully unloaded $14 million of the $17 million in non-allowable real estate investments. However, one $3 million property remains on the books, given the economic environment. Despite the fact that the proposed investment would enable the thrift to meet the 8 percent risk-based requirement, the application cannot be approved until all nonincludable investments are sold. The institutional investors, as limited partners in the proposed investment, will not execute capital maintenance agreements nor are they willing to grossly over-capitalize the institution to accommodate the OTS. The result: the investment has been lost, and an otherwise healthy institution may create a further burden on the taxpayer through another RTC resolution.

Another example: A limited partnership is prepared to recapitalize a billion dollar institution with $22 million worth of equity. This recapitalization will result in full compliance with only two of the three capital ratios. The risk-based capital requirement is projected to be in compliance within nine months of the transaction. The regulators rejected the deal. The reason: the risk-based capital requirement will not be met the day the deal is consummated and the limited partnership will not sign a capital maintenance agreement. The end result: $22 million is kept outside the industry.

A third example: A stock thrift has fallen out of compliance with current requirements. Certain existing shareholders have agreed to infuse additional capital to bring the institution into compliance. Through this infusion, these shareholders would increase their percentage of ownership to a position of control. Thrift Bulletin 5a now requires either additional capital to meet the "fully phased in" requirement or a capital maintenance agreement. The shareholders will not agree to either. The result: no new capital and a greater risk of an insolvent institution.

These three examples demonstrate how regulatory rigidity is keeping precious capital away from the thrift industry. In two instances alone, $120 million which was slotted to be invested in the thrift industry has been lost. The only reason for this failure is rigid application of regulatory standards. The potential result of this rigidity is that the taxpayer will foot the bill. The regulator should make capital intention easier, not more difficult. The downside to the taxpayers is minimal. With proper examination and supervision, the only real downside is to the investors who inject these funds into undercapitalized thrifts. The upside involves providing a greater cushion to possible future losses in these thrifts as well as improving their profitability. (Greater capital, by definition, implies greater profitability since those funds can be invested to yield interest income.) This ultimately protects the U.S. taxpayer.

No one is advocating a system where undercapitalized operators would acquire marginal institutions with little or no capital risk. Nor is it advantageous to have a system that operates on a case-by-case basis without guidelines for approving recapitalization applications. Inept or dishonest management of financial institutions cannot be tolerated, and scarce capital cannot be dissipated. Tax avoidance deals and expensive yield maintenance agreements are clearly inappropriate. However, Thrift Bulletin 5a and the requirement for capital maintenance agreements prevent badly needed capital from providing protection to the deposit insurance fund and the U.S. taxpayer, and appear to conflict with the purpose of FIRREA: enhanced capital levels.

II

The Survivors: Strategic Success Paths

Assuming that profit opportunities will determine the nature of the thrift business in the future, the key question thrifts and other depository institutions are asking is: what are the profit opportunities available to thrifts that will shape the future form of the industry? The industry in its present form will be eliminated because the initial reason for its creation ceased to exist. Thrifts were established in order to provide long-term financing to American home owners. Toward that end, they were given a monopolistic quarter percent differential on their savings rates. That regulated rate differential provided a steady stream of low-cost, longer-term savings funds into the industry. These funds were used to make fixed long-term mortgages to home owners.

With the lifting of Regulation Q, which abolished the rate differential on the liability side, and with the development of a nationwide brokered deposit market, the thrift's ability to fund themselves cheaply and with stable deposits has vanished. At the same time, the introduction of the secondary mortgage market facilitated by Freddie Mac, GNMA and Federal National Mortgage Association (FNMA) eliminated the unique role that thrifts have played in mortgage origination. Anyone could now lend long-term money, securitize it and sell it off, thus taking it off their books and eliminating the interest rate risk associated with longer-term assets. The unique position which thrifts occupied on both the asset and the liability side was lost. With it, the reason for their existence has been eliminated. Thus, the future of the industry depends on each institution's ability to convert into a new strategic position, which will not necessarily depend on its traditional role.

Several alternative strategic positions are available to today's thrifts in their quest to identify a defensible strategic position for the future. Practical strategic planning tools can and should be used in order to select the strategic alternative best suited to a specific thrift's position. Several of these tools and their applications are described later in this book.

One key to successful strategic selection is leverage. Venturing out into new businesses where none of a company's strengths are brought to bear is a strategy which has a high likelihood of failure. Each thrift has unique strengths. Examples of such strengths include a customer base, thriving market, management skills, technology, economies of scale/size, strong technical skills, broad product line, market recognition, and leadership. Selecting your strategic position will be most effective if your company's strengths are utilized to crest a competitive advantage in the strategic preposition selected. For example, a strong, loyal customer base and perception of community orientation can be parlayed into a successful community banking strategy.

At the same time, leverage does not mean that one must have all the requisite skills necessary in order to make a strategy successful in-house. In fact, if, for example, leveraging your customer base means a broader product line, it may be critical to success to use outside people who are experienced in the new products you intend to introduce. If you believe that insurance is a product which is needed by your customers and which you can market effectively, recognize that insurance is best sold and managed by experienced insurance industry people. Your own staff may not be easily convertible into the team necessary to achieve success. Qualified leadership from outside the institution is often key to success in new product introduction.

Several main strategic alternatives seem to be the most likely success choices for thrifts today. This section will describe three likely alternative positions which may present the greatest leverage opportunities and likelihood of success to today's and tomorrow's thrift institution. The three strategic success paths offered here are aimed at leveraging the strengths and competitive advantages typical of successful thrifts. Community banking is designed to capitalize upon the thrift's loyal customer base and long-term relationships, as well as its solid community standing as a civic leader and good corporate citizen. Mortgage banking can leverage a thrift's origination network and experience, as well as the techical knowledge of the residential real estate market. Consumer lending is designed to utilize the thrift's strong customer base and the mortgage loan as an anchor to a diversified relationship.

This section describes each of these businesses, their fundamentals and critical success factors, to help you assess the relative attractiveness of each business and its potential fit into your company. In addition, practical tools that will help you decide which of these (and other) alternatives best fit your institution are provided.

5

Community Banking: Expanding into a Full-Service Retail Depository Institution

Introduction

Thrifts typically have strong customer loyalty. Many have developed deep roots into their communities and to their customers throughout the years. These thrifts can parlay those strengths into a viable community banking strategy, thereby serving their community fully with an emphasis in retail banking to consumers and small businesses.

Many skeptics, however, question the viability of community banks, and ask whether they are an endangered species. It has been rumored that community banks are dinosaurs whose time has passed.

It is widely recognized that the banking industry is quickly becoming the financial services industry. With this transition come economies of scale, product diversification, and many other changes that, some say, little community banks cannot accommodate. In the new banking industry, it is said, there is no room for the "mom and pop" shop. Figures are cited to support this assertion. For example, it costs the average small bank over $180 per year to process a credit card while it costs Citibank under $60. Other lines of business such as mutual funds and installment loans also seem to be scale sensitive, thereby being perceived as the exclusive domain of large banks. Finally, the technological requirements to operate the business are becoming increasingly complex and expensive. An obvious assumption some make is that a small player cannot compete effectively in this environment. In a time where bottom-line performance is more important than ever, the small community bank cannot produce profitable results in a world where size and sophistication are critical to success.

The demise of the community bank was most eloquently—and mistakenly—predicted by McKinsey & Co. in 1985. That study suggested that there would be 100 banks in the United States by the year 1990. This prediction obviously did not come true, as today we have over 12,000 banks and thrifts. In fact, de novo banking has been stronger than ever until the last two years. In New Jersey there were more new charters granted in 1989 than ever before. Similarly, Pennsylvania approved more new charter applications in 1989 than the combined total for the past 25 years. The strength of de novo banking is of particular significance since the requirements for granting new charters are tougher than ever with greater minimum capital requirements ($8 million), harsher scrutiny of the proposed management, and tougher criteria for demonstration of community need. Why are these banks popping up now when they are characterized as obsolete? Are these new bankers deluding themselves into believing they have something to offer that their big brothers cannot?

New community banks are being created to meet real needs which are not met by the larger banks. Many community banks thrive by filling in the void created by consolidation. Although they may not maximize cost efficiencies or offer a wide range of sophisticated services, community banks provide other benefits which customers are prepared to pay for. The assumption implicit in the predictions of their demise—that cost is the overwhelming consideration for purchasing banking services—has been proven unfounded by the prosperity and long-term survival of the community bank.

Community Banking Is Here to Stay

The reasons for the survival of the small banks are many. Historically, the U.S. banking system was designed to prevent concentration of financial power into few hands. This is why the dual banking system was created. Unit (not branch) banking was established and interstate banking prohibited, among other measures, to ensure diversification of financial power. This bias for the entrepreneurial spirit has not vanished and is exhibited in many industries. The respect for Yankee ingenuity coupled with fear of monopolies and large conglomerates is widespread all across the country. This attitude, in turn, fuels the demand for the small bank survival to prevent concentration of financial power.

Consolidation has created a small group of very large banks, but it also bred a new generation of small competitors. This phenomenon occurred in many industries that experienced significant consolidation, but it is especially true for service businesses. In such industries service is indeed a critical component of the product delivered, and it often suffers when consolidation takes place. Personnel and facilities' duplication result in layoffs. Such a move often brings about the destruction of many well-established, long-term relationships built between the community banker and his or her customers.

Certain customers are not prepared to trade off the lower service levels for greater efficiency, lower cost of service, or broader product line. These customers seek the personal attention and advice they were accustomed to. Only the community business-oriented institution can meet their needs.

Accounting and law firms are excellent examples of industries where the very large co-exist with the very small. These two industries each meet the needs of different customer bases and offer different service levels. Both are viable in their own markets. A large accounting firm is less likely to give a small business the same level of service it provides its largest prime clients. The additional product diversification often accompanied by size is not especially relevant to the small business whose needs are fairly limited in the first place.

The same is true for banks. Large banks are hard pressed to be as community oriented as the small community banks. Although large banks may employ local people, their turnover is typically higher and their overall interest is lower than community banks. Conversely, for the local bank their community is all there is. Consequently, the bank's interests, level of knowledge and community relations reflect that. Community banks can be much more responsive to situations which require handling that is not by the book. The community bank is tied to its community. Its commitment to the community is unquestionable. The larger bank's business is much more defined by unemotional economics and numbers which, in turn, may render certain communities less viable or attractive when their economies experience difficulties. The members of the community know that and often prefer to deal with a bank that is here to stay.

Although the community bank cannot possess the same technological capabilities as larger competitors, the rapid decline in the cost of technology makes it affordable even to smaller players. Imaging technology, for example, is used by banks as small as $80 million in assets. Similar examples abound. Hence, the small bank can still capitalize upon certain technological features. For instance, vendors offer a myriad of features and services that the smaller bank can contract through outsourcing rather than owning. It broadens its product offering and customer responsiveness. Mutual funds, trust services, investment management, loan participations, asset securitization, and many other services can be contracted out in a way that makes the size of the community bank transparent to its customers.

In contrast to these arguments, there is a downside to community banks which may indeed diminish their numbers during the 1990s. Simply stated, many are not viable business entities. Size is a factor, particularly as the role of automation and technology in banking becomes more critical and the size of the community (and its bank) cannot support the necessary infrastructure. A community bank ties its fortunes to the economic conditions of the community. The inevitable lack of diversification results in extreme vulnerability of the bank to local economic downturns, as was evidenced by both large and small banks that did not foster economic diversification in Texas and New England. Smarter, larger banks ensure that as they consolidate, their local unit is minimally altered. These branch offices are then in a position of offer a competitive alternative to the small stand-alone community bank. Although this strategy may be more expensive than gutting the local newly acquired bank, it also is more likely to provide continuity and enhance customer retention.

Certain customers may outgrow their banks; their needs become more sophisticated or geographically diversified and the local bank can no longer meet them.

These and many other reasons explain my conviction that we will see a further reduction in the number of small community banks. Although the need for the community bank is strong in many areas and although they provide a unique service package, not all community banks will be able to survive as consolidation continues and the economics of the business get even tougher.

Another major reason for the survival of community bank is that they have continuously proven themselves to be profitable practical institutions. Underscoring the profit potential of small institutions, an *American Banker* survey has found that the most successful community banks were twice as profitable last year as the average U.S. bank.

The 100 most profitable community banks with assets between $50 million and $500 million earned an average of 2.04 percent on assets, the survey found.

The most profitable community banks with assets of less than $50 million did even better, posting a 2.2 percent return. By comparison, the average U.S. bank's ROA was 0.91 percent. But, while specific comparative data were not available, the returns of the top performing community banks clearly exceeded those of their larger counterparts (see Table 5–1).

One important reason for this high profitability is cost consciousness and productivity, as measured by pretax operating income per employee. The leader among small community banks, First National Bank, Johnson, Nebraska, in 1990 racked up $137,000 of operating income per employee, compared with $15,350 for the average U.S. bank employee.

Another common attribute of many top performing community banks was a high concentration of interest-free demand deposits. The most profitable small

Table 5–1: The Most Profitable Community Banks
(based on return on average assets in 1990)
(Industry average is 0.22)

Bank	ROA
Republic Bank, Norman, OK	3.6%
First American Trust, Santa Ana, CA	3.5
First National Bank, Ely, NV	3.3
First Bank of Immokalee, FL	3.3
Bank of Talmadge, Talmadge, NE	3.0

community bank—Republic Bank—had 23.4 percent of its liabilities in noninterest bearing accounts (see Table 5–2).

Despite the over capacity of the industry, community banking is a viable strategic alternative for survival in the future. Its success is rooted in our country's culture and is a logical profitable path for thrifts looking for a strategic identity in the future. Today the quality of service and personal attention as well as the ability to customize transactions command a premium. Consequently the viability of a thrift's conversion into community banking hinges on its ability to deliver the quality of service and level of attention the customer demands.

What Is Community Banking?

Community banking is an approach to the customer. It is not necessarily a function of size. A community bank is one that derives most of its funding from the communities it serves (as opposed to purchased funds) and invests these funds into the same communities (although that is not a necessary condition). Given this definition some large banks, such as Marine Midland and Old Kent, fall within the community banking category, as do large thrifts such as Georgia Federal. However, other attributes of the community banking approach to the customer differentiate

Table 5–2: The Top Performing Community Banks
(1990 performance ratios)

	Return on assets	Return on equity	Noncurrent loans as a % of assets	3-year assets growth
100 most profitable small community banks	2.22%	15.90%	0.67%	21.60%
100 most profitable large community banks	2.04	18.71	0.74	36.80

large banks from the small ones. These attributes which are key to the success of the community bank include the following:

1. *Customer Decisions Made at the Local Level.* Both asset and liability prices are determined at the local community bank level. This approach allows the bank to tailor its pricing structure to the competitive conditions in its market. For example, if the average cost of funds is low in the local market, the community bank's liability prices will reflect that cost rather than the nationwide levels of CD rates. Local pricing of loans is even more important because it permits the flexibility of customized deals and recognition of special relationships or unique circumstances. Thus, community banking requires decision-making authority at the local level.

2. *Relationship Building.* The anchor of the strong community bank is the relationship of its chief executive, the officer team, and its employees to the community. One-on-one relationships with target customers and prospects is key to success. Using services, pricing, and customized transactions to cement their relationship, the community banker brings a unique dimension to banking services. Banks that do not foster the community banking approach cannot compete with it.

3. *Strong Community Involvement.* Executives and employees of the community bank are deeply involved with their community through charities and civic leadership positions. This involvement not only makes them more effective business developers but also reflects their true interest in a commitment to their community. They donate their time, and on occasion the bank's money, to the advancement of the community within which they operate. This commitment is becoming increasingly important to the customer as evidenced by many consumer surveys. Respondents to the *American Banker* 1990 and 1991 consumer surveys expressed strong preference for local institutions and for banks with high Community Reinvestment Act ratings, both of which reflect the extent to which the bank reinvests its funds in the community and is committed to the economic welfare of the community.

4. *Limited Product Line.* The community bank typically offers only basic banking services. This product line not only allows management to do what it does best, which is fundamental banking, but also fully meets the needs of most of the

community bank's customers. However, the limited product offering (resulting from the institution size) is a competitive disadvantage to attracting some customers. Thrifts have learned that sticking to their knitting is not necessarily bad. Many thrifts have achieved and maintained their profitability by doing what they do best: real estate finance on the one hand and deposit services on the other. However, those that perceive that real estate finance is insufficient in order to maintain profitability in an intensifying competition market may choose to expand their product line and add a variety of commercial banking services without compromising the community orientation.

People Are Critical of Successful Community Banking

Community banks exhibit several characteristics in their human resources management that enable them to maintain and strengthen their presence and profitability.

1. *Minimal Turnover.* The community bank, unlike most large banks and the merger-oriented banks, offers continuity of service personnel. The customer develops a relationship with the account officer, the teller or the branch manager and the relationship provides a strong anchor because the same person takes care of the customer's needs year in and year out. The high turnover that has characterized merged institutions in recent years is making this attribute of community banking more important than ever in creating a competitive advantage.

2. *Accessibility of Senior Management.* One of the great advantages of community banking as perceived by customers is the ability to reach top management, including the president. No customer is too small for a small bank's president. This availability gives the customers a sense of importance, of being a significant client of the bank.

In addition, senior management has the authority to respond quickly to the customer's needs and to bend the rules if necessary. The increased flexibility and timely turnaround are significant assets to the community bank's competitive position.

3. *Organizational Identity and Staff Commitment.* A community bank often resembles a family much more than any banking institution. The resultant low turnover has already been mentioned. However, other benefits are also accrued from the community bank's distinct organizational identity, including low absenteeism and a willingness throughout the employee ranks to go the extra mile. People who work for community banks typically know their institution's mission, its target market, and the level of service that is expected. They are treated better than the employees of many other large and impersonal organizations. In turn, they respond with equal loyalty and a commitment to the bank and its customers.

4. *Team Approach.* Most community banks are cohesive units. Everyone is moving in the same direction and all share a purpose. Politics are minimal, particularly as compared to large organizations. Many "win" situations exist. Employees depend on each other's performance to fulfill the customers' needs and to get their own reward. This type of pressure results in increased cooperation. The team approach not only makes the community bank a nicer place to work but also enhances the effectiveness of its employees because everyone operates as a team rather than at cross purposes.

Community banking is defined here as an effective approach to handling customers. Although it is not the only effective approach available to banks today, it is a viable strategic alternative for small banks and for thrifts that seek to find their niche in an increasingly competitive industry. Doing what they do best, offering the highest level of service and intense personal attention to their customers, is still the strongest attribute of community banks which will permit them to occupy a defensible strategic position in the future.

Many banks reorganized the benefits of community banking. As a result, we are also seeing the emergence of a new institution: the super-community bank. Seven hundred of its kind are already in existence and doing very well. These are banks that grow in order to achieve critical mass and economies of scale yet consciously emphasize their local presence and flavor despite the additional costs incurred. Back office functions are consolidated, including accounting, purchasing, payroll, human resources, data processing, financial management, treasury, asset/liability management, and strategic planning. However, these benefits are all transparent to the customer. Local staffing remains stable, decision-making authority remains at the local level, and most and often both the local presidents and the board are retained. It is possible that these super-community banks are the answer to the profitability questions raised by today's scale considerations. Either way, the community bank is a long-term survivor in the industry and rumors of its extinction are premature.

Key Success Factors

What should the CEO of a community bank do in order to successfully implement its strategy? The following elements are important:

1. *Strategic focus.* Know what your bank is in business for and have a clear definition of your strategy. In community banking the strategy has a geographic parameter to it. Know how far you want to go and whether your community orientation applies only to the liability side (generates deposits locally but buys assets elsewhere), or to the asset side as well (generate deposits locally and reinvests the money in the community lending to individuals and businesses). The strategic focus should include the product line you plan to offer. Community banks often limit their product line to plain vanilla banking. However, if your community is predominantly affluent, or aging, or young and upwardly mobile, the bank may need to customize the product line to the specific community. For example, aging customers typically are not credit intensive but have a greater need for savings and investment products of all kinds. They may be interested in mutual funds and other investment instruments. However, one should bear in mind that the risk propensity of older customers is low and therefore esoteric investments products such as global diversification mutual funds are unlikely to attract their attention. By the same token, older people typically have substantial equity invested in their home and may be good candidates for home equity lines of credit. This is but one of the examples of customizing and tailoring the bank's product line to the population in its target market. The product line of both deposits and assets should mirror the needs of the community, which vary by the type of people resident in the community, the demographics, the economic welfare, key industries, and the like.

2. *Control.* Make sure that the bank's risks are well managed, with particular emphasis on asset quality and credit risk. These are the non-negotiables of the business. One major bad loan can wipe out the bank's equity in no time, or at minimum, damage profitability for an entire year. Therefore, asset quality is of the highest importance and should be a focal point of the CEO's activities.

A well-controlled bank in terms of the variety of risks that it incurs is a profitable bank. Among the elements that should be manage tightly are asset quality, interest rate risk, liquidity risk and regulatory risk. When managing interest rate risk, the bank should recognize that variable rate assets do not eliminate interest rate risk. If all loans are variable rate, that does not mean that the bank does not bear interest rate risk. The risk eliminates from the *relationship* between the assets and your liabilities. Therefore, if the assets are repriced overnight (prime-based loans for example) yet liabilities are repriced much less frequently, such as fixed-rate 3-year CDs, a major interest margin squeeze will take place when rates go down.

Therefore, interest rate risk should be consciously managed to minimize volatility of earnings as well as to control the volatility of the value of portfolio equity (the fixed-rate mortgages and the bonds in true loan and investment portfolios). Managing interest rate risk is not only required by the regulators but is also important in order to enhance profitability, stabilize stock prices, and attract future capital into your institution. Steady performance and controlled growth are more important than star years followed by occasional poor performance.

3. *Numbers.* Manage your bank by the numbers. Impose financial discipline on your people. Clarify your expectations and set them up front so that all managers know what they are expected to do and have financial, quantifiable measurements to success and failure.

Managing the performance of the bank by the numbers is a productive and easy way to enhance control and improve profitability. In community banking, five numbers would be sufficient to understand the profitability dynamics of the institution as a whole. These numbers are net interest margin, loan loss provision, other income, operating expense, and operating profit. Essentially, net interest margin less provision plus other income less operating expense equals your operating profit (see Figure 5–1).

Figure 5-1 Managing by the Numbers

Net interest margin

− Loan loss provision

× Other income

− <u>Operating profit</u>

= Operating profit

By setting in advance the required operating profit in terms of return on assets as a basis (identified as a percent of assets), one can quantify each of the elements, (the margin, provision, etc.) as a percent of assets and understand which component needs adjustment. This simplified view of the bank's profitability dynamics clearly depicts whether operating expenses could be sufficiently covered by the core earnings of the bank (net interest margin) and to what extent the company is dependent on other income in order to generate the required profits.

4. *Entrepreneurship.* In a community bank the entrepreneurial spirit is the spirit of the bank. Therefore, initiative taking is essential to success, and reward for that initiative is a part of that success. Initiative and creative thinking should be rewarded even when not entirely successful. An overly risk-adverse culture will result in hesitancy on the part of staff to think creatively and come up with new solutions to customers' problems. Instead, they will stick to proven paths of action and forego new opportunities. If failure is penalized severely and there is no room to make mistakes, initiative taking in the institution will be minimized. Take the good with the bad, within limits, and reward initiative.

Teamwork is also important, but it must entail clear individual responsibility of all team members. Otherwise team work may degenerate into "decision by committee" which essentially implies inaction. Without clear individual responsibility, team members will not know what they are called upon to do and how they will get rewarded for their performance. Consequently, the choice course of action for them would be paralysis. Teamwork is an important component towards making the whole greater than the sum of the parts. That is why lines of accountability and responsibility within the team are essential to its success.

5. *Reward.* Reward performance in a timely manner and make the rewards significant enough to motivate people to give their most and to serve the customer. Rewards do not necessarily mean monetary rewards. Company-wide recognition and psychic rewards are equally important, if not more important, than monetary rewards to some people. Some people find a pat on the back or recognition more important than a significant bonus. Others want you to save the praise but put your money where your mouth is. The rewards should be customized to the individual if at all possible in order to maximize motivation. The rewards you give should be timely and send a clear signal to the individual that he or she had done well.

Acquisitions and Super-Community Banking

Acquisition Philosophy

Community banking does not exclude the possibility of acquisitions, particularly if the company is planning to become a super-community bank. As a super-community bank, acquisitions are an integral part of the growth strategy and of future success. When acquiring, there are two essential principals to keep in mind:

1. The consolidation process needs to be streamlined and standardized to ensure an effective and timely consolidation. Every newly acquired institution knows what to expect in terms of lines of authority, responsibilities, support from corporate headquarters, and layoffs. One must ensure that the community banking corporate culture permeates throughout the institutions acquired. It is critical that the same culture is observed throughout the company. This will minimize discord and will ensure that all resources are operating in a consistent manner, thus improving efficiencies and productivity.

2. A savings target should be set for each acquisition and the acquisition managed to achieve that target. This is an extension of the "manage by the numbers" principle which can be successfully applied to acquisitions. However, as a super-community bank, one should be cautious in setting cost savings goals. These should not jeopardize the level of customer service and should be realized in areas that are transparent to the customer.

As the organization proceeds through acquisition, it should not lose sight of the primary purpose. A strong CEO is important in providing leadership, and stability. Unnecessary product diversification should not be undertaken lightly because it is in vogue. Fads in our business have traditionally been at the root of industry-wide crises. Fads ranging from Real Estate Investment Trusts and thrifts' service corporations, to third world debt and leveraged buy-outs brought nothing but trouble to the financial services industry. Other fads such as discount brokerage proved ineffective in making a *significant* impact on the bottom line. Therefore, sticking to a clearly defined strategic focus in terms of geography and product line and avoiding fads is effective management. Fads often only divert management's attention from the areas where it can indeed get the most bang for the buck. Managing the margin and select fee income opportunities which respond to the customer's needs are more likely to yield stable profits and ultimately give you the greatest return on your investment.

The Super-Community Bank Structure

There are four areas of responsibility within the super-community bank: corporate management, product lines, operations, and bank and branch distribution network.

1. Corporate Management

Corporate management involves the following areas of responsibility and activities:

◆ Shareholder value

◆ Strategic focus

◆ Strategic planning

◆ Corporate-wide marketing

◆ Capital

◆ Company-wide controls

◆ Mergers and acquisitions

◆ Asset quality

◆ Corporate culture

◆ Company-wide risk management

Effective Management Results: Company-wide strategic focus

2. *Product Lines*

Product lines involve the following areas of responsibility and activities:

◆ Cost efficiency

◆ Product quality

◆ Service responsiveness

◆ Product management

Effective Management Results: Low cost production

3. *Operations*

Operations involve the following areas of responsibility and activities:

◆ Systems design and development

◆ Operating design and development

◆ Distribution design and development

◆ Market and customer information

◆ Re-engineering

◆ Quality initiatives

◆ Policies and administration

Effective Management Results: Improved margins and reduced risk.

4. *Branch Distribution Network*

Bank and branch distribution network involves the following areas of responsibility and activities:

◆ Franchise development

◆ Sales culture

◆ Service quality

◆ Customer needs

◆ Local pricing

◆ Local marketing

◆ Community orientation

◆ Marketing strategy and implementation

Effective Management Results: Enhancement of franchise value.

The Super-Community Bank Strategic Position

Some medium size banking companies are out to disprove one of the widely held assumptions of the merger wave: The future belongs only to the very large, efficient banks and to very small, service-oriented community banks. Not accepting the notion that they may be too small to be big and too big to be small, this emerging breed is adopting an identity of its own, the super-community bank. A growing number of multi-bank holding companies are striving to meet the super-community bank definition. They seek to combine the centralized operating efficiency and product standardization that are characteristic of many big banking companies with a decentralized management that makes key pricing, lending, and marketing decisions in and for local communities. These companies have good reason to try to preserve the community focus even as they grow into multi-billion dollar networks.

A survey of 125 super-community banks showed that these institutions outperformed the industry. They averaged 0.88 percent return on assets in 1990, which is 38 basis points better than the industry as a whole as calculated by the Federal Deposit Insurance Corporation. These banks can also readily outperform others in quality and customer service. Because they gain the benefits but lose the drawbacks of both bigness and smallness, super-community banks are a competitive threat to big and small institutions alike. About half of the 125 super-community banks in the survey have less than $1 billion in assets. These banks averaged a return on assets in 1990 of 0.92 percent up from 0.90 percent the year before.

On the other hand, many of the super-community institutions are very large. One prime example is Banc One Corp. in Columbus, Ohio. It has over $50 billion in assets and earned 1.53 percent return on assets in 1990 and 1.73 percent in the third quarter of 1991. Banc One has expanded rapidly through mergers, but it prefers to leave the acquired managements in place while giving them decision-making autonomy with clear performance parameters. The holding company imposes its high performance customer service, technology applications, product, time, and financial reporting standards on the acquired bank in order to transform good banks with good management into great banks with great management. John B. McCoy, Banc One's Chairman, describes Banc One as a "people first institution"; it thereby epitomizes the super-community ideal. Super-community banks also have local presidents and local boards of directors in all banks. It works.

While many in the industry are going in the opposite direction towards consolidation and centralization, particularly through mega-mergers, the super-community bank remains close to its roots. The larger the super-community bank gets, the more cautious it should be not to think as a super regional. "If you start thinking like a super regional, you start sliding away from the local community orientation. As the president of such a large company, it would be easy to slip into the $10 billion mode and forget about these 50 million branches in the country. By so doing, the super-community bank can lose its competitive advantage," said McCoy. Anything that affects the customer should be left to the local banks' discretion. Super-community banks cite local orientation and autonomy as the principal benefit of not consolidating. Functions that are centralized are most likely to be staff functions, like operations that are transparent to the customers. For example, while 93 percent of the super-community banks surveyed had centralized data processing, only 44 percent centralized loans.

There are two main criteria when deciding on centralization versus decentralization.

◆ How much can you save if you centralize?

◆ What is the impact on the level of service and the products and services delivered to the customer?

Many super-community banks choose to keep loan underwriting resident in the banks, regardless of the size of the total company. It keeps them more customer sensitive.

Why Super-Community Banks Will Survive

A recent report entitled "Vision 2000," a report on the future of banking by Arthur Andersen & Co., Andersen Consulting, and the Bank Administration Institute, was based on discussions with senior bank executives and other experts. It predicted the emergence of the super-community institutions that would maintain the look and feel of a close to the customer community bank but leverage their size and strength to provide a full range of products. The report predicts their size will reach up to $25 billion in assets.

"Vision 2000" further predicts a 25 percent decline in the number of domestic banking entities to 7,300 by the turn of the century, but that the number of organizations with $1 to $25 billion in assets, namely the super-community banks, will rise. In the *American Banker's* 1990/1991 National Consumer Surveys, two of three respondents said they would prefer to bank at a local or community institution. Among small town and rural residents, 77 percent expressed that preference in 1991, compared to only 59 percent in the cities and suburban areas where personal attention is less expected. Thrifts who are close to their customers are particularly well suited to successfully implement this strategic position.

No two super-community banks are alike. There are gradations in the autonomy granted to subsidiaries, managements, and boards. Some assign those boards nothing more than honorific functions. A few do not keep separate presidents in place, but for the most part super-community bankers' scales tip toward decentralized autonomy, at least in product.

Local banks have a built in advantage. They are focused on a town, their attentions are not diluted, and there is no internal debate about what they should be. But if a larger bank defines itself as a community bank and does it right, it will be just as tough as a locally owned bank.

What Is a Super-Community Bank? A Definition

Strategy

Super-community banking is a three-pronged strategy (see Figure 5–2). It is designed to create an institution that combines the best features of both small and large banks. On the one hand, the super-community bank is not too big to offer the warm, friendly service for which community banks are well known. On the other hand, it is not too small to realize significant cost efficiencies and offer the broad product line which only larger institutions can offer. The cornerstone to the strategy is community banking service levels, which are typically offered through an unconsolidated multi-bank holding company structure. Each bank has its own president and board, and keeps decision-making as close to the customer as possible. At the same time, the holding company strives to "make the whole greater than the sum of the parts" by expanding the product line across its individual banks and creating cost efficiencies which do not penalize customer service levels throughout the system. The following are the three elements of super-community banking:

◆ Strong community orientation

◆ Customer-transparent cost savings

◆ A broad product line

Figure 5–2: Super Community Banking

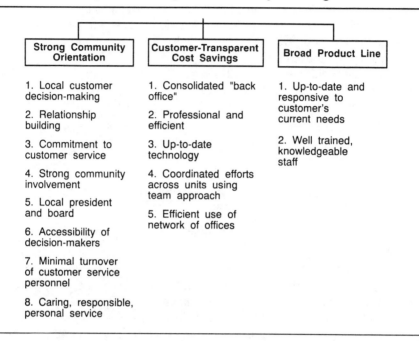

Strong Community Orientation	Customer-Transparent Cost Savings	Broad Product Line
1. Local customer decision-making	1. Consolidated "back office"	1. Up-to-date and responsive to customer's current needs
2. Relationship building	2. Professional and efficient	2. Well trained, knowledgeable staff
3. Commitment to customer service	3. Up-to-date technology	
4. Strong community involvement	4. Coordinated efforts across units using team approach	
5. Local president and board	5. Efficient use of network of offices	
6. Accessibility of decision-makers		
7. Minimal turnover of customer service personnel		
8. Caring, responsible, personal service		

This strategy is unique in that it provides defenses against large and small banks, builds value in the franchise, and generates strong profits.

Characteristics

The characteristics of the super-community bank are designed to achieve the best of the large and small bank's position.

I. Community Orientation

Local Decision-Making. Local decision-making authority and strong ties to the community are critical to success. Hence the presence of the local president and support of a board comprised of local community leaders are important components of the super-community bank.

While the boards and president represent a layer of overhead that could otherwise be eliminated, they also represent the bank's commitment to the community and to the service implications of that commitment. Reduced customer turnover and greater pricing flexibility represent the return on that investment.

Local presence also facilitates growth of local market share through the use of the president's and board's local contacts.

Customer Accessibility. Another major competitive advantage of community banks is the accessibility of senior management and other decision makers to customers of all sizes. Small and large customers alike can speak with the department head and the president to gain access to the decision-making and transaction flexibility which only the senior management level can exercise. The super-community bank ensures that those characteristics do not get lost in the process of creating a larger holding company.

Much like the smaller community bank, the super-community banking organization strives to retain employees at the local level and maintain continuity of customer contact.

The larger banks and regionals merge other institutions into their banks. They follow this transaction with major turnover and maximizing cost efficiencies.

Commitment to Continuity. But the super-community bank is committed to keeping service continuity at each bank's level. Therefore, mergers into a super-community bank are less painful to the smaller bank management, since most personnel are retained. This is particularly true for customer service personnel.

Another benefit to this continuity is enhancing the bank's ability to fully understand its customers' need and to design its product line and delivery systems to meet those needs.

The super-community bank normally does not centralize the decisions on customer pricing. The focus of each pricing decision is not the transaction itself but the customer. The super-community bank, therefore, remains close to the customer and maintains authority and control of pricing decisions under the executives of each bank.

Pricing Flexibility. Although coordination is important—and sometimes essential, especially in the case of overlapping markets—the guiding philosophy is to leave the flexibility of the pricing structure, both deposits and loans, at the local level.

Decentralized Oversight.

- ◆ Separate president in each subsidiary   90%
- ◆ Separate charters for subsidiaries   88%
- ◆ Separate board of directors   85%

(Responses by 125 holding companies in survey)

This approach takes full advantage of the community banking element of the super-community bank, since it allows each bank's president and executive team to customize their pricing and transactions to individual customers and their market conditions.

Certain guidelines from the corporation may be imposed on each bank, particularly regarding liquidity levels, credit quality, asset quality, and fees.

The purpose of these guidelines is to ensure that each bank acts consistently with the corporate objectives towards maximizing asset quality and increasing profitability.

Relationship Orientation. By the same token, decision-making autonomy at the individual bank level is essential to retaining the customer service edge. This is key to the success of the super-community bank and to maintaining the customer franchise.

The super-community bank is always geared toward building a relationship, as opposed to a transaction orientation. It is interested in attracting and then retaining the customer. Strong customer retention is followed by increasing cross-selling activities and declining acquisition costs. The bank is not interested in maximizing the fees of one transaction. Rather, it is a long-term approach to maximizing profits. Consequently, the management of each institution spends an extensive amount of time catering to customers and prospects, marketing at the local community level, and building the relationships.

Flexibility in transactions structuring and pricing as well as quick turnaround time—which results from investing decision-making authority at the local level—come into play in building the relationship.

Focus on Service Quality. Service quality, a key element to achieving customer satisfaction and retention, is another major attribute of the super-community strategy. It is the small bank-like service level that the super-community bank is committed to offer, thus offsetting one of the important competitive advantages of small banks.

The individual members of the super-community bank maintain close involvement in their own community. The board, chief executive, and senior management team of each member bank get involved in a wide range of community-oriented activities. They strive to maintain civic leadership and participate actively in charity and other events that demonstrate their commitment to the local community.

That commitment serves to defend their market position relative to both larger and smaller banks, while leveraging resources already available to the bank in each community.

II. Broad Product Line

As mentioned earlier, the concept of the super-community bank is based on a three-pronged strategy. A broad product line is a cornerstone of the strategy. It is important to offer a wide array of products and services that will meet the customers' needs so that customers will not outgrow the bank and customer retention will be achieved. This is one purpose of the franchise and a way to maximize its value.

The super-community bank does not leverage the franchise at the expense of the customer service level. Rather, it strives to maximize revenues through the franchise by combining effective relationship-building with a broad, sophisticated product line. This combination provides the winning formula for defending the super-community bank against the small bank's service, since smaller banks cannot offer the product breadth and sophistication that can only be supported by a larger asset base.

By the same token, that combination defends against the larger bank, which can offer the product sophistication but loses the personal service and relationship-management aspect. The effectiveness of this element of the strategy hinges on the bank's ability to offer training so that the staff is both knowledgeable and sales oriented. The quality and salesmanship of the staff are essential to improve the leverage of existing resources, including distribution channels and customer bases.

III. Cost Savings

The super-community bank does not aim to maximize the cost effectiveness of a large asset base. In other words, it does not attempt to minimize human resources costs and centralize all operations and decision-making activities to maximize savings. Rather, it strives to reach a balance between cost efficiencies and relationship management.

This trade-off is typically achieved by centralizing functions that are transparent to the customer, ranging from accounting and investments to loan processing and other data processing functions. Processing activities offer significant scale savings. At the same time, they are transparent to the customer. Hence, the consolidation of back-office processing functions provides an effective tool available to the super-community bank to take advantage of its size without sacrificing the community-banking orientation.

Scale Sensitive Technology. Technological investment is another scale-sensitive element to the strategy. Technological innovations represent high fixed cost. The greater the volume of assets over which the cost is spread, the greater the efficiency. In addition, technology can be used to improve customer service and sales effectiveness. Platform systems and imaging are two prime examples of such applications. They permit faster service and turnaround time, while facilitating cross-selling and warm personal service.

Most super-community banks have a clear vision of their strategy and the desired market position. That vision is shared throughout the ranks. Employees and management alike understand the purpose of the bank, its philosophy, and culture. This commonalty goes a long way to increase staff productivity and to motivate employees at all levels to go the extra mile and be their best. Caring, responsive personnel is also conducive to creating a team approach whereby all resources are moving in the same direction. This, in turn, increases the effectiveness of resource utilization and promotes consistency across the individual bank.

Using the office network as a coordinated mechanism to generate low-cost deposits and efficiently distribute products is another aspect of the leverage element of the strategy. "Production" of deposits, interest income, fees per square foot, and fees per employee are all important measures of that leverage and its success.

The super-community bank attempts to combine the important characteristics of small community banks and large banks. It takes the community banking approach to the customer from the small bank and combines it with some measure of cost efficiencies, which are created by economies of scale and the breadth of product offering from the large banks. That combination is a winning strategy for the banking industry in the 1990s. Many smaller banks see the super-community bank structure as a major threat to their existence. Rightly so. In many cases, a super-community bank can offer service that is equal—if not superior—to the smaller bank, thereby nullifying the smaller bank's primary competitive advantage.

The super-community bank is not only a friendly acquirer of smaller banks. It can also be used as a vehicle to maintain the existence of many small banks, while leveraging their capabilities through a central structure of costs and products. Thus, the super-community bank may not only be the threat, but also the solution, to the successful survival of many small banks.

Many community banks will continue to survive and prosper as standalone units throughout the United States. But it is unlikely that all 11,000 of them will survive this decade. One alternative available to community banks that perceive their competitive position to be indefensible in the long run is the formation of a super-community bank with other similar institutions in their marketplace. In effect, community banks use the super-community structure as a defensive strategy against acquisition, as well as a way to enhance shareholder value. By joining the super-community bank structure, it is likely that their profitability and franchise value will improve. This will fulfill the fundamental obligation to shareholders, while taking full advantage of existing management skills and community ties.

In Search of Quality and Customer Retention

Another key ingredient to the success of community banking is quality service. It is the primary competitive advantage of community banks which cannot be well emulated by larger competitors. Those thrifts who select community banking as that strategic anchor must ensure that the quality of their service meets these expectations.

The definition of quality varies greatly. Bank and thrift customers generally say they are satisfied with their financial institution. They cite factors such as friendliness, speed, accuracy, empathy, and responsiveness as describing quality. Customers give their primary financial institution high grades for specific aspects of the relationship, but have qualms about the overall quality.

This fact is of great importance when one considers the penalty for low quality service. Sixty-five percent of bank defections are caused by service-related reasons, rather than by price or cost-related reasons. People change their banking relationship when their complaint was not handled properly and courteously. They are less likely to switch for 50 basis point of additional yield on their CD. In fact, long-term customers are less likely to switch for 100 or even 200 basis points in yield differentials. This, of course, could mean significantly wider margins for community banks with loyal customers.

Bank changes due to quality problems are most frequently found among those customer segments which are most attractive. For example, in the sought-after 35-44 years old group, 56 percent said they will switch banks due to quality problems (as surveyed by *American Banker/*Gallop 1991 Consumer Survey). 59 percent of those with incomes exceeding $70,000 said the same. Poor quality service results in customer defection. The price for such defection is high, since customer acquisition costs are not insignificant. It costs five times as much to acquire a new customer as to sell a service to an existing customer.

Quality service is also directly related to customer retention, which, some say, is a critical component in bank profitability. The longer a customer stays with the bank, according to Bain & Co. consultants, the greater the profitability of the account due to increasing balances, multiple accounts, lower operating costs (one customer information file contains several accounts and relationships), acceptance of lower yields and higher loan fees, and referrals of new customers. This concept is under significant debate, but is intuitively appealing.

Further, quality service generates customer satisfaction, thereby increasing customer retention. In addition, customer satisfaction also generates employee retention, since it contributes to employee pride and makes the day-to-day job easier and more pleasant. The greater the employee satisfaction, the longer the employee stays with the bank. Employee retention translates into lower costs (we all know that hiring new people is costly both in terms of search fees and transaction costs as well as in terms of absolute compensation levels and training costs) and higher service quality (provided by a motivated, knowledgeable employee). These, in turn, increase customer satisfaction, and this wheel of success continues.

Improved retention is said to reduce the cost of funds and increase deposit balances. Quality service is the way to achieve customer retention. There are many elements which can be managed in order to achieve the level of service needed to maintain or increase customer retention. Among these are the following:

◆ *Service Philosophy.* Make a clear, unwavering commitment to service. "Customer is king" should be the motto in the organization, and service levels should be an obsession of all employees.

◆ *Product Line.* Expand the product line as needed to ensure that customers get what they want, rather than what you think they want or whatever services are covenient for the bank to offer. Meeting customers' needs is the first way to achieve customer satisfaction.

◆ *Pricing.* Pricing may be out of line with the competition. If pricing is too low, raising fees is appropriate, but the marketing and handling of such changes is key. If prices are too high, lowering them should receive maximum exposure in the marketplace.

◆ *Training.* "Simple schools" such as the Disney school truly work! Training staff to provide the service levels unique to community banks is effective; they need the guidance and model behavior to emulate.

◆ *Performance Measurement.* Including service levels or customer satisfaction in performance measurement is an excellent motivator. Mystery chopper programs and customer surveys are good information and data collection tools to assess whether each employee is delivering the service quality the bank is looking for.

◆ *Incentives.* Incentives create motivation, and can be used effectively in motivating quality service and desired behavior. It is important to understand the full range of the customers' preferred delivery systems and to strive to offer all desired alternatives to the customer base.

◆ *Organization Accountability.* Quality has to have a champion. Like other organization initiatives, it will die without institutional support and individual responsibility.

Managing these and other relevant elements will bring the service levels at the bank to the quality level which the customer expects. Achieving and maintaining such quality levels will, in turn, increase customer loyalty, and through it contribute directly to the bottom line of the company.

Thrifts have traditionally been considered by their customers to be caring, service-oriented institutions. They have embedded goodwill, which they can capitalize upon in their transition into a full community banking institution. The quality service dimension is the cornerstone of the strategy, and could become the key to a successful transformation.

A Case in Point—A $42 Million Thrift Which Turned into a Community Bank

While traditional S&Ls deal in residential mortgage loans, certificates of deposits and securities, Horizon Savings, an Austin, Texas thrift, is a true community bank. It specializes in making Small Business Administration guaranteed loans, interim loans, and commercial real estate loans. Horizon has to survive under the shadow of the largest banks in the country, including NationsBank and Banc One. It identified a niche for itself which, it believed, the large players are not interested in and are less equipped to handle successfully. Recognizing its inability to compete directly with the big banks and their delivery systems on mainstream banking, the thrift turned into community banking with a focus. Horizon specializes in one-to-four family construction loans. It is currently doing business with 75 percent of the top builders in its market. The thrift also moved into the credit card business, which it subsequently sold for a substantial profit.

Horizon is one example of the growing industry-wide realization that "the walls are tumbling down." Banks are seeking to expand their presence in the thrifts' mortgage business and thrifts are moving into community banking. The majority of thrift institutions already consider themselves community banks today, as evidenced by their response to a nationwide survey conducted by BDO Seidman. They identify with community lending rather than residential mortgage lending as they have in the past. Although many will still probably be specialists in home lending, the majority of thrifts are committed to serve the full range of consumer's financial needs through consumer loans. Many thrifts are also committed to other kinds of lending in the community such as small business loans.

Thrifts today have to look at their markets and decide where the opportunities lie. Horizon Savings Association of Austin did so. It is but one example of hundreds of thrifts that recognize they need the flexibility to examine their own markets and identify a new business focus for themselves, often within the parameters of community banking. The resulting trend is that banks and thrifts are getting into each other's business, which will ultimately result in a homogeneous depository institutions segment. The difference among institutions will be by business focus, not by charter. Thrifts today essentially enjoy the same powers as banks and have consistently described themselves as banks in recent years, not only for marketing purposes but because they truly perceive themselves to be quite similar to banks. Consumers also view banks as a generic term, with little perceived differentiation between thrifts and commercial banks.

Horizon savings is a great example of something that looks, feels and smells like a community bank. Its commitment is to the local community, and its product line reflects that commitment beyond the traditional residential mortgage business. Horizon returned 1.5 percent on assets in 1991, and its tangible capital ratio is 5.62 percent.

6

*Consumer Lending: Expanding Beyond Residential Real Estate**

The extension of consumer credit and diversification of types of consumer credit are natural expansions of the traditional thrift's business. Thrifts have traditionally been collateral based lenders. They used real estate as collateral to make long-term loans to individuals. Their primary customer base was and still is individuals, not businesses. As a result, thrifts that have been successful in making mortgage loans and in developing a loyal customer deposit core have a natural base from which to grow a thriving consumer lending business. They already have the customer relationship. They may wish to leverage that position and expand the relationship to include other types of credit beyond residential real estate.

The potential for consumer credit growth is significant. The overall share of savings institutions of that market has been declining (see Table 6–1). Out of $730

---

*This chapter relied on information provided by George H. Hempel, Alan B. Coleman, Donald G. Simpson, in *Bank Management* (New York: Wiley, 1990.)

69

Table 6–1: Consumer Credit by Holder, in Millions of Dollars

Major Holder	August 1991	August 1990
Commercial banks	$335,662	$340,525
Finance companies	135.509	139,496
Credit unions	92,843	93,071
Savings institutions	37,893	51,822
Retailers	37,296	39,557
Gasoline companies	4,857	4,722
Pools of securitized assets*	87,471	67,287
Total	**731,531**	**736,480**

Figures include automobile and mobiule home loans, revolving credit, personal loans, and home improvement loans.

*Outstanding balances of pools upon which securities have been issued; these balances are no longer carried on the balance sheets of the loan orginator.

Source: Federal Reserve Board

billion of consumer credit, only $38 billion are held by savings institutions as compared to commercial banks, finance companies, and even credit unions, which have at least triple the thrifts' share of the consumer credit market. In addition, a growing segment of consumer credit holders are pools of securitized assets. The phenomenon of securitization will be discussed later. It is of critical importance as it is changing the fundamentals of the consumer lending business.

Thrifts have been precluded from diversifying the types of consumer lending they did beyond residential real estate. Their balance sheets demonstrate that (see Table 6–2). However, now that they are permitted by law to expand their basis and capitalize upon the natural competitive advantage they have in the extension of consumer credit, the question is how to successfully enter other types of consumer lending, and which types are right for each individual institution? What are the strategic avenues available to them to successfully expand their business?

Definition

The primary type of consumer loan is installment credit. This type of credit came into its own only after World War II. At that point millions of consumers were eager to buy new cars, household appliances, and other durable goods that had not been available during the war. As a result, the level of installment lending in the United States rose from an insignificant $2.5 billion in 1949 to $29 billion in 1955. In 1988 outstanding installment credit from all categories of lenders stood at $625 billion; by August 1991 that figure had jumped to $732 billion.

The postwar growth of consumer lending is the result of the steady rise of income and employment and the increased perception of job security across America. Growing and secure future income is key in the extension of consumer credit because buying on time means acquiring goods with tomorrow's income. In part, the growth of consumer lending also reflects the aggressive marketing by banks and other financial institutions in competing for the consumer loan market. In order to compete more effectively, they created new instruments and forms of credit, including credit cards, overdraft facilities, long-term revolving lines, and longer loan maturities. All were designed to make credit more attractive and more available to consumers.

Consumer lending continued to grow by increasing lender penetration into the consumer market and distribution of credit to more and more households. The percentage of households having installment debt has been rising continuously across all age and demographic categories. It concentrated not just in younger families.

Since the mid–1970s consumer credit has grown faster than personal income, resulting in a sharp rise in the ratio of consumer credit to disposable income. Some industry observers are concerned that the debt capacity of consumers is at risk of being exceeded and that we are overstretching ourselves. Consumer credit to personal income stood at 5 percent in the mid–1970s and peaked at 19 percent in 1986. Others feel that the risk is minimal since many households have high liquidity in the ratio of installment credit outstanding to the amount of consumer held liquid assets has remained around 20 percent for the past two decades. Consumers are using credit for purchasing a broad range of goods including recreational activities and luxury items. Concurrent with this development is the rise in consumer debt delinquencies and personal bankruptcies (see Figures 6–1, 6–2). The changes do not necessarily imply major future losses for banks and thrifts. They do, how-

Table 6-2: Selected Financial Institution Balance Sheet Items as a Percentage of Total Assets*

Item	1988[1]			1986[2]			1985[3]			1984[4]			1983[5]			1973[6]		
	S&L[a]	MSB[b]	CB[c]	S&L	MSB	CB	S&L	MSB	CB	S&L	MSB	CB	S&L	MSB	CB	S&L	MSB	CB
1. Cash, federal funds, and investment securities	13.5	17.4	28.2	13.0	24.7	30.9	13.2	34.3	30.5	12.8	36.5	31.5	12.9	27.9	35.8	7.8	27.0	40.1
2. Residential real estate loans	56.9	53.3	14.2	55.8	49.1	10.3	56.5	40.7	10.1	64.1	40.6	10.6	67.1	51.5	9.3	76.5	57.1	8.9
a. 1-4 family residential	35.7	37.4	10.4	38.4	35.5	8.4	43.3	34.9	8.4	46.2	34.6	8.6	51.4	34.8	8.2	67.3	45.0	8.1
b. Multifamily residential	5.7	5.8	.7	5.5	5.2	0.6	6.6	5.7	0.5	6.4	6.0	0.5	5.6	8.0	0.4	8.4	10.3	0.8
c. Mortgage-backed securities	15.5	10.1	3.1	11.9	8.4	1.3	9.8	n.a.	1.1	11.5	n.a.	1.5	10.1	8.7	0.7	0.8	1.7	n.a.
3. Business credit	14.4	18.3	30.1	16.5	14.5	28.1	16.4	13.6	28.2	10.7	12.5	28.4	8.0	11.5	26.4	8.0	11.8	24.1
a. C&I loans	1.9	4.7	18.7	1.7	4.0	19.0	1.4	3.9	19.8	0.8	3.2	20.6	.2	2.4	19.6	0.1	0.3	19.5
b. Commercial real estate	12.6	13.6	11.4	14.8	10.5	9.1	14.9	9.7	8.4	10.0	9.3	7.8	7.8	9.1	6.7	7.9	11.5	4.6
4. Consumer loans†	4.4	5.2	12.5	4.2	5.8	12.6	4.0	5.6	12.4	3.1	4.6	11.5	1.3	3.4	9.2	0.6	1.8	10.8
5. Other loans	1.1	.7	7.7	1.2	1.2	9.1	1.1	1.0	9.1	1.0	1.4	9.1	1.6	1.1	9.7	1.2	0.2	12.2
6. All other assets	9.7	5.2	7.3	9.4	4.6	9.0	8.9	4.6	9.6	8.3	4.2	8.8	9.1	4.6	9.2	5.9	2.1	4.0

Source: Jim Burke and Stephen A. Rheades, "Commercial and Consumer Lending by Thrift Institutions," *Journal of Commercial Bank Lending*, May 1991, pp. 15–24.

* Total assets are adjusted for unearned income on loans for all years and possible loan loss provisions as well for 1983 and 1973

^a Savings & Loans   ^b Mutual Savings Banks   ^c Commercial Banks

[†] Before 1984, consumer loans exclude loans for retail model homes and home improvement.

[1] Using June 30, 1988, Call Report data based on 13,214 banks with adjusted total assets of $2,635 billion, 375 MSBs with adjusted total assets of $233 billion, and 3,145 S&Ls with adjusted total assets of $1,448 billion.

[2] Using June 30, 1986, Call Report data based on 14,128 banks with adjusted total assets of $2,398 billion, 353 MSBs with adjusted total assets of $165 billion, and 3,284 S&Ls with adjusted total assets of $1,221 billion.

[3] Using June 30, 1985, Call Report data based on 14,329 banks with adjusted total assets of $2,208 billion, 265 MSBs with adjusted total assets of $140 billion, and 3,332 S&Ls with adjusted total assets of $1,142 billion.

[4] Using June 30, 1984, Call Report data based on 14,366 banks with adjusted total assets of $2,005 billion, 270 MSBs with adjusted total assets of $136 billion, and 3,184 S&Ls with adjusted total assets of $992 billion.

[5] Using June 30, 1983, Call Report data based on 14,500 banks with adjusted total assets of $1,947 billion, 386 MSBs with adjusted total assets of $165 billion, and 3,206 S&Ls with adjusted total assets of $256 billion.

[6] Using June 30, 1973, Call Report data based on 13,842 banks with adjusted total assets of $762 billion, 483 MSBs with adjusted total assets of $106 billion, and 4,129 S&Ls with adjusted total assets of $256 billion.

n.a. = Item not available on the Call Report.

Figure 6–1: Number of Loans Delinquent as a Percentage of Total Number of Loans Outstanding

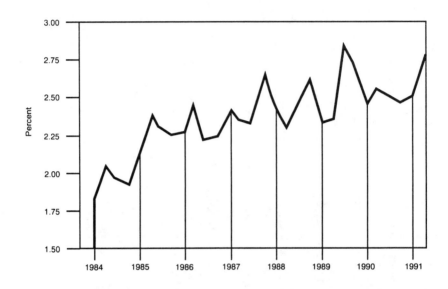

Source: American Bankers Association. Reprinted with permission from *Consumer Credit Delinquency Bulletin.* All Rights Reserved.

ever, underscore the need to control consumer lending underwriting standards carefully.

The number of loans delinquent as a percentage of total number of loans outstanding has increased fairly steadily since 1984 on all types of loans. Even during recession when retail sales are flat, credit card outstanding were increasing at double digit annual rates. The implication is that people are using available credit card balances to supplement their ordinary income and to keep their level of purchases going. The trend resulted in a sharp increase of credit card delinquencies in 1991.

Competitive pressures to make consumer loans is likely to accelerate as commercial lending opportunities continue to be scarce. Given that scenario, even a modest increase in consumer credit demand would include proportionally riskier loans. But it seems that commercial banks would rather assume the risk of consum-

Figure 6–2

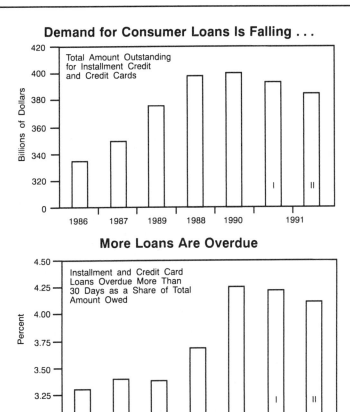

Demand for Consumer Loans Is Falling . . .

More Loans Are Overdue

Source: FDIC

er loans, which are generally collateralized, than on corporate loans with their much greater exposure and lack of credit diversification. As competition intensifies, thrifts that are contemplating entering the business or expanding their presence in it should continue to adhere to their profitability hurdles and credit underwriting standards in order to ensure the uncompromising creditworthiness of the portfolio and the ongoing profitability of the business. It is a seductive concept to cut rates and temporarily reduce spreads in order to build share. It may even work. But the risks, particularly if underwriting criteria are compromised in the process, could be significant.

Types of Consumer Credit

Credit Card and Debit Card Lending

Credit card overdraft loans seem to promise the highest rate of consumer debt growth in the future (see Table 6–3). This type of lending is based on preauthorized lines of credit that can be drawn down as the consumer makes cash purchases from any of more than 1.5 million merchants who accept such cards. The easy access to credit through plastic cards has been dramatically facilitated by the rapid expansion of electronic banking services, such as automatic teller machines and point of sale terminals at merchant locations. The temporary hampering of credit card lending through state usury laws was lifted in the late 1980s when these restraints were modified and liberalized in many of the states, making credit card lending one of the most potentially profitable activities in the business.

Automobile Lending

Direct car loans are loans made to consumers for the purchase of a car, where the car serves as the collateral securing the loan through a chattel mortgage. Indirect car loans are those loans acquired from car dealers. In these cases the consumer applies to the dealer for a loan. The dealer, in turn, conveys the information regarding the consumers creditworthiness to the bank. Turnaround time on such decisions must be very quick since the dealer is interested in selling the car. Indirect auto lending requires special relationships with the car dealers and in-depth understanding of the customer profile of the intermediary, namely the auto dealership.

In the dealer relations of may banks it is understood that the individual loans in a package will vary in quality. Dealers are often permitted a certain number of marginal creditworthiness buyers for the size of loan or collateral value involved. As a result, delinquencies and losses on indirect automobile loans might be twice as high as those on direct loans. In addition, banks pay car dealers rebates on the loans they provide. Indirect car lending is more risky and requires much more expertise that direct automobile loans.

Automobile debt rose for several decades. It has recently declined at commercial banks because of the aggressive low market rate financing by the automobile

Table 6–3: Types of Consumer Credit

1. The Business' Consumer Lending Portfolio Tops $60 Billion

For 2,949 federally insured savings institutions with $1.35 trillion in assets as of December 31, 1988; dollars in millions.

	Loans on Deposits
Outstandings	$3,662
Share of total consumer loans	6.01%
Share of total assets	.27%
Number offering	2,874

2. Consumer Loan Emphasis Varies by Asset Size

By asset size as of December 31, 1988; dollars in millions

	Loans on Deposits

Under $100 million
Total numbr of institutions: 1,462   Total Assets: $70.6 billion

	Loans on Deposits
Outstandings	$514
Share of total consumer loans	15.55%
Share of total assets	.73%
Number offering	1,415

$100 million–$499 million
Total numbr of institutions: 1,064   Total Assets: $231.6 billion

Outstandings	$1,007
Share of total consumer loans	9.95%
Share of total assets	.43%
Number offering	1,043

$500 million–$999 million
Total numbr of institutions: 180   Total Assets: $126.5 billion

Outstandings	$448
Share of total consumer loans	7.94%
Share of total assets	.35%
Number offering	176

Over $1 billion
Total numbr of institutions: 243   Total Assets: $922.8 billion

Outstandings	$1,694
Share of total consumer loans	4.04%
Share of total assets	.18%
Number offering	240

Source: *Federal Home Loan Bank Board,* quarterly reports
(Table continues)

Table 6–3: Continued

Home Improvement Loans	Education Loans	Auto Loans	Other Closed-End Loans	Credit Card & Other Open-End Loans	Mobile Home Loans	Consumer Financing Leases	Total
$4,518	$3,951	$14,717	$12,817	$13,313	$7,347	$653	$60,978
7.41%	6.48%	24.13%	21.02%	21.83%	12.05%	1.07%	100.00%
.33%	.29%	1.09%	.95%	.99%	.54%	.05%	4.51%
1,957	1,108	2,087	2,221	1,381	1,044	80	2.926
$368	$101	$712	$1,054	$269	$280	$6	$3,304
11.13%	306%	21.54%	31.91%	8.14%	8.48%	.19%	100.00%
.52%	.14%	1.01%	1.49%	.38%	.40%	.01%	4.68%
808	356	896	998	418	395	16	1,443
$1,161	$715	$2,488	$2,669	$1,306	$734	$36	$10,115
11.48%	7.07%	24.60%	26.39%	12.91%	7.25%	.36%	100.00%
.50%	.31%	1.07%	1.15%	.56%	.32%	.02%	4.37%
794	495	824	852	619	388	26	1,060
$460	$381	$1,175	$1,371	$1,131	$583	$91	$5,639
8.15%	6.76%	20.84%	24.31%	20.05%	10.33%	1.62%	100.00%
.36%	.30%	.93%	1.08%	.89%	.46%	.07%	4.46%
146	98	154	158	141	98	10	180
$2,529	$2,754	$10,342	$7,723	$10,608	$5,751	$519	$41,920
6.03%	6.57%	24.67%	18.42%	25.31%	13.72%	1.24%	100.00%
.27%	.30%	1.12%	.84%	1.15%	.62%	.06%	4.54%
209	159	213	213	203	163	28	243

Source: *Federal Home Loan Bank Board,* quarterly reports

manufacturers. Both direct and indirect lending on new automobiles were hurt by this development. The maturities of both types of loans has consistently increased as car finance companies now often offer 60-month loans on new cars. In 1988, average maturities ranged between 55.9 months for new cars and 46.8 months for used cars and interest rates ranged between 2 to 2.5 percent over prime rate for new cars and as much as 5 percent over prime for used cars.

Home Equity Loans

Home equity loans have been a popular product with savings institutions given their expertise in real estate. Home equity loans involve large personal revolving lines of credit that are secured by the equity in the borrowers' homes. Borrowers typically access the line through checks. The home equity loan gained wide popularity in the middle 1980s and received a special boost due to the Tax Reform Act of 1986. This law curtailed the deduction of interest on other consumer loans, including auto, credit card, and other non-mortgage loans. The deductibility of interest on mortgage type loans including home equity lines continued to be valid. As a result, the after-tax cost of home equity credit declined relative to the after-tax costs of other types of consumer credit. From the banker's standpoint, home equity lines replaced car loans, which declined dramatically at times during the 1980s.

The benefits of home equity loans are many. They offer the bank a collateral which has appreciation potential, as opposed to car loans where rapid depreciation is par for the course, and credit card loans where no credit is offered and personal bankruptcies often imply a total write-off of the loan. A 1987 survey found that the average house supporting a home equity loan was appraised at $101,000, whereas the average outstanding balance of the first mortgage was $39,000, leaving substantial equity available to be financed. In addition, the loan to appraised value limit applied by the average bank providing financing was 77 percent, indicating an additional $39,000 that could be borrowed. Thus the potential for the growth of home equity credit is significant. Thrifts are particularly well suited to offer this product given their expertise in real estate.

Mobile Home Financing

Mobile home financing is quite similar to car loans. Most mobile home financing is indirect, that is arranged through dealers. Banks add floor plans inventory financing for the dealer to their product line in order to induce the dealer to do business with them. Mobile home financing experienced rapid growth in the 1960s and 1970s with the explosive growth of the industry. The continually high cost of conventional housing suggests that mobile homes will continue to grow. However, the relative poor credit quality of this market has resulted in a decline in mobile home lending by commercial banks. Many mobile home borrowers do not have strong credit histories, and default and delinquency rates on such loans are relatively high. As a result, compared with conventional home mortgages, mobile homes have shorter maturities—typically seven to 12 years—and interest rates which are 4 to 5 percent higher than conventional mortgages.

Consumer Lending by Savings Institutions

Before 1980 thrift institutions were restricted by law to making only mortgage loans. This resulted in institutions with long-term assets and short-term liabilities, as well as major concentrations in real estate lending. As the problems of such a balance sheet structure became evident in the late 1970s, Congress passed legislation in 1980 and 1982 that expanded the asset powers of thrifts. This legislation allowed them to make commercial and industrial loans as well as consumer loans. These powers, along with the authorization to offer transaction accounts, made thrifts much more like commercial banks in terms of their potential powers.

A decade has now elapsed since the thrifts were granted new powers. How have their balance sheets changed? In 1973 thrifts held only 0.2 percent of their assets in commercial loans. This compared to almost 20 percent of the commercial banks' assets. Similarly, they held only 1.2 percent of their loans in consumer loans, as compared to 10.8 percent for banks. By 1983, three years after Congress first expanded the asset powers of savings institutions, they had made only minor inroads into commercial and consumer lending. From 1983 to 1988 the percentage of thrift-generated commercial and consumer loans of the total asset mix has continued to increase. The most marked increase was in consumer loans; mutual savings banks held as much as 5.2 percent of their assets in such loans. Thrifts have indeed expanded their consumer lending activities. On the other hand, they have not grown their commercial lending activities significantly.

The regional differences in terms of leverage opportunities indeed seem to lie with the consumer, not commercial, activities. The diversification of thrifts into non-traditional lending are presented below.

Trends in Consumer Lending in the 1990s

Consumer lending in the 1990s is encountering new and constantly changing obstacles as well as opportunities. For example, savings institutions are offering a growing variety of consumer loan products. At the same time, the competitive scene is intensifying. The overall volume of consumer loans as described before has skyrocketed. Savings institutions' share of the total market increased from 1980 to 1988 from less than 5 percent to 10 percent. The market itself has grown 140 percent. This upward trend is expected to continue into the 1990s, particularly as the economic realities of the mortgage market may shift some additional emphasis to consumer lending. We now not only have overcapacity in the mortgage market but a very efficient secondary market which has driven down the yields on mortgage loans. Consumer lending, given those circumstances, may be one of the great hopes for the future of the thrift business.

Risk-based capital considerations, on the other hand, are creating a disincentive for thrifts to make consumer loans. The risk-based capital rate of consumer loans is 100 percent, compared 50 percent for a one- to four-family home mortgage. Offsetting the regulatory impediments to consumer lending is the interest rate risk management component of the business. Consumer loans offer variable rate and shorter terms loans, thereby widening the variety of maturities's available to thrifts in managing their interest rate risk and their balance sheet.

In addition, savings institutions should consider other trends, such as securitization and bulk product sales. These new alternatives may ensure that consumer lending remains a profitable activity within any regulatory environment by permitting the originating institution to keep the fees and a certain spread, but to sell the asset, and with it, both interest rate risk and capital exposure.

Related Products

Consumer lending as a profit center also brings the opportunity for related products that can be sold to the borrowers. Examples of these products include credit insurance, life and accidental health insurance, and mechanical breakdown insurance. The following elements are key success factors for a related product program strategy.

1. *A Distribution System.* With branches in place, thrifts are ahead of the competition in that they could potentially sue their employees to sell fee income producing products. However, some thrifts' employees may not be convertible into salespeople. They may be too used to a passive mode of operations where they are order takers, as opposed to aggressive initiative-taking salespeople. Depending upon the makeup of each institution's staff, hiring new employees specifically for their sales ability may be a necessary component.

2. *Flexible Effective Products.* A good product menu with a variety of choices is essential in selling the right product to the customer. The products offered should be customer driven and designed to meet the full range of customers' needs.

3. *Training.* Effective training for employees is a critical step in the process. Employees must understand the products in order to see them effectively and meet the customers needs. Without such training, regardless of incentive programs, they will be less effective in selling related services.

4. *Incentives and Motivation.* Bonus programs and other incentives are necessary to reinforce and reward desirable performance. This is particularly true for the traditional thrift employee who had been used to being measured solely on the basis of deposit volume. This is a new and different product line, and proper incentives must be put in place for the traditional thrift employee to sell the service and not perceive such sale as detrimental to deposit gates.

5. *Commitment.* A high initial level of commitment and an effective follow-up program by top management are necessary to any successful program launch. Without such commitment, any new program will wilt and die under its own weight.

Offering the related products has many other benefits in addition to the potentially highly desirable fee income. The more services the customer buys, the more solidified is the relationship. Strong relationships and cross-selling activities are key to success.

Interest Rate Charges and Consumer Allowance

Add-On Rates

The rate on car loans and most other types of consumer installment loans are quoted in terms of an add-on rate (see Table 6–4). That rate is applied to the

Table 6–4: Interest Rates for Several Types of Consumer Credit

Type of Credit	Rate
Home equity line of credit	10.2%
Credit card	17.9
New car loan (48 month)	10.5
Personal loan (24 month)	14.2

Source: "Home Equity Line of Credit," *Federal Reserve Bulletin* (June, 1988), pp. 361–373.

original loan principal base charged over the life of the loan, despite amortization of the principal through the installment payments. For example, if an 8 percent rate is quoted on $1,200 one year loan that is to be paid monthly the interest amount of $96.00 ($1,200 x 8 percent) is added up front to the amount borrowed, and the monthly payments are determined by dividing principal plus interest for $1,296 by 12 (the number of payments). The resulting effective annual rate is nearly 16 percent, or double the add-on rate quote. When more than one payment is made over the life of the loan the add-on rate will always result in an effective rate that is higher than the nominal rate. This reflects that fact the borrower does not have full use of the amount borrowed for the whole time period. The more frequent the installment payments, the higher the effective rate. These facts must be disclosed in accordance with truth-in-lending legislation and regulations.

Bank Discount Rate

An alternative method for calculating interest is one which considers the amount loaned equal to the amount to be repaid minus the interest amount. If the principal is $1,200, to be borrowed at 10 percent and repaid after one year, the interest amount would be $120. Using simple interest, the $120 would be the interest paid for the use of $1,200 over the entire year. In the bank discount method, however, the $120 would be deducted from the $1,200, leaving $1,080 to be used for the year. The effective interest rate in this case would be much higher. This method is sometimes used for single payments consumer loans and for small business loans. Once again regulations require the bank to disclose the true annual percentage rate.

State Usury Ceiling

Installment loans, credit card loans, and other revolving loan rates are typically subjected to state usury limits. These are specified limits on add-on as well as true annual percentage rates imposed by the state. In the middle and late 1980s a temporary federal preemption of state usury laws was put into effect.

Variable Rate Consumer Loans

In the early 1980s variable rate pricing for installment loans became popular in response to soaring cost funding in an era of high and volatile interest rates. Wide acceptance of variable rate pricing among corporate customers was not followed by consumers' acceptance. A prolonged period of generally falling rates beginning in 1984, however, won over consumers to variable rates. As a result, variable rate installment lending dominated fixed-rate lending in the early 1990s by a considerable margin. Overall, consumer preference for fixed- or variable-rate loans will depend upon current rate levels and rate expectations of rate movements.

Prepayment Penalty

Prepayment penalties are an important source of revenues. The bank is entitled to collect more than the interest that would be prorated to the length of time the loan is outstanding in the case of prepayment because of the high average loan balance during the early part of the loan period and because the bank incurs an origination cost that originally was intended to recover during the full life of the loan. The usual approach to determine the customer's rebate is the rule of 78 method. Under this method the rebate amount varies according to the time at which prepayment occurred, and is based on the sum of installment period numbers. The finance charge in any month when prepayment occurred will be a proportion of the sum of the months digit over the maturity of the loan. For a 12-month loan the sum of the digits will be $2 + 3 ... + 12 = 78$, hence the term, the rule of 78. In this case, the bank's total charge for the first month will be 12 times the amount charged in the 12 months. 12 over 78 for the total finance charge is earned over the first month, 11 over 78 in the second month, etc. This rule is sometimes criticized as being arbitrary and unfair to the borrower.

    The mathematically accurate method of computing loan prepayment charges is called the actuarial method which calculates the earned finance charges on the actual (declining) balances before prepayment occurred. This method is quite complicated and time consuming and in most cases the rule of 78 method fairly approximates the actuarial method. The rule of 78 is not a good approximation of the annual percentage rate when interest rates are very high, or the loan maturity is unusually long.

Credit Analysis of Consumer Lending

Credit quality is the number one determinant of the potential profitability of any loan. This also holds true for consumer loans. The problem is that consumer loans involve the handling of a large volume of customers. Each borrower represents a relatively small loan, and the bank needs to process a great many of them to generate a substantial dollar volume of nonmortgage consumer loan business. With such large numbers of borrowers, it is vital that bank management exercise effective control over the consumer credit granting process. The thrifts' experience in mortgages is both a benefit and a hindrance in entering consumer lending. Although the experience in collateral-based lending is valid and could be transferred, the processing efficiency is entirely different due to the much lower balances and the much higher number of borrowers.

Efficiency is key to a successful program. Most lenders with large numbers of consumer applications supplement individual loan-by-loan credit analysis with sophisticated credit scoring. This automated analysis system can be used to evaluate applications using a scorecard that lists application characteristics, such as income level, job tenure, status of residence, and established credit with retailers or other lenders. The application is awarded point values for each characteristic; and the total points indicate whether or not the application should be approved. Acceptability is predicated on the bank's data base of past applicants with similar credit worthiness profiles and the delinquencies incidents among these applicants.

Credit scoring is seldom used as the sole criteria for granting consumer credit. Other factors, such as debt payment capacity, present financial condition, collateral requirements and repayment history, must all meet the bank's underwriting standards. Subjective information, such as character, the potential for a profitable relationship in the future, and other unquantifiable factors makes credit analysis a judgmental process. It is a process whereby both quantitative and qualitative information are evaluated simultaneously. The end objective of the process is to minimize loan losses and nonperforming loans.

Consumer Credit Analysis

Typically, the process of consumer credit analysis involves the following steps:

1. Determine loan purpose and amount.

2. Obtain information.

    ◆ Consumer credit application

    ◆ Personal financial statement

    ◆ Income tax returns

    ◆ Business financial statements

3. Investigate and verify information.

4. Analyze the data gathered

    ◆ Cash flow

    ◆ Financial statements

    ◆ Collateral evaluation (if applicable)

    ◆ Credit evaluation systems

5. Evaluate collateral if applicable.

6. Price and structure the credit.

1. Determine Loan Purpose and Amount

During conversations with the applicant, the purpose of the loan and the amount needed are determined. The type of loan, such as checking, revolving line of credit with overdraft convenience, large personal revolving line of credit including home equity credit or installment loans (both short- and long-term), or a single payment loan is reviewed at that time as well, and the final loan type and structure are determined.

2. Obtain Information

As in mortgage lending, the most valuable credit information available in consumer lending is supplied by the loan applicant. The applicant must provide information on the bank's standardized credit application form which includes data on employment, income, housing, marital status, assets owned, and outstanding debt. It is prudent to require a current personal financial statement on unsecured loans and on large secured loans. It is also prudent to require income tax returns and business financial statements on self-employed applicants.

An important secondary source of credit information is the credit reporting agencies. These agencies make it their business to collect extensive data on consumers' credit histories, including listing of outstanding debts, legal actions and promptness of payment. They compile these data from information supplied by creditors. Regulation B governs the way in which creditors maintain their customers' credit records and how they report the records to credit agencies or other inquirers.

3. Investigate and Verify Information

Before depending on the information provided by the borrower it must be verified. Personal financial statements are typically prepared. They should be tested for accuracy and how realistic they are, hence, how true they are. Direct verification is often made by contacting present employers and creditors about reported indebtedness. In terms of collateral investigation, legal searches should be conducted to determine the presence of any previous claimants who filed under the uniform commercial code. Appraisals on both real and personal property may be required to establish an estimate of collateral values. A successful thrift mortgage lender can use procedures similar to those currently utilized in mortgage collateral verification to verify collateral for other customer loans.

Information and Equal Credit Opportunity. Under the Equal Credit Opportunity Act (ECOA) and regulation B, borrowers have the right to withhold certain information that they perceive as irrelevant to the loan transaction. Due to the complexities of regulation B, it is not always clear what information bankers are not permitted to require of the borrower. Most banks model their loan application form after a standard form published by the Federal Reserve Board that conforms with the regulation requirements, thereby ensuring compliance.

4. Analyze the Data Gathered

Cash Flow Evaluation. Unlike mortgage lending where the collateral is a major source of repayment, cash flow analysis is even more key to the ability to repay consumer loans, particularly when unsecured. The lender looks to the cash flow as the primary source of repayment. The collateral pledged is merely a secondary source of repayment and is used to reduce the risk and to help define the amount of the loan. It is not the basis, per se, for making the loan. This feature is somewhat different from mortgage lending.

Financial Statement Evaluation. In analyzing the personal financial statement, the assets shown must be reviewed to assess their liquidity. For example, underwriting standards for credit line loans sometimes require liquid assets to equal or exceed the amount of the lien. Diversification of assets is another important component to provide more stable net worth. The borrowers' tangible net worth must be calculated and intangible assets ruled out. Credit line borrowing may require tangible net worth to be three or more times the amount of the credit line. The borrower's total income should be from stable and dependable sources. Secondary and collateral sources should also be determined. The borrower's financial status is important in structuring the loan to fit the borrower's payment capacity and needs. When collateral is called for, the loan should be structured with an appropriate collateral value margin.

Ultimately, the primary concern in consumer loan analysis is to identify the specific source of repayment. The usual source is income from wages. This requires an evaluation of the employment stability and of other claims on the income such as debt payment obligations and a reasonable level of subsistence. The process of determining whether adequate resources are available to repay the loan invoices cash flow analysis. Calculating the debt to income ratio is a major component of the analysis. The ratio compares the regular sources of income exclusive of contingency or unverified income to fixed monthly obligations. These include mortgage payments, installment and charge card payments, child support, etc. Many banks require that debt-to-income ratio does not exceed 40 percent. Again, experience gained from prudent successful mortgage underwriting can be applied to the debt to income ratio analysis and benchmark.

Credit Evaluation Systems. In collateral-based consumer banks, the value of the collateral should be verified, as the collateral is the main secondary source of payment. Appraisal, sale price, or industry statistics are all appropriate sources for collateral assessment. In general, however, it is the borrower's ability to repay that should determine the loan decision. The collateral serves to enhance the lender's position and reduce the risk of loss if default occurs.

5. Evaluate Collateral if Applicable

Judgmental Credit Analysis. The judgmental system of consumer credit analysis relies on the experience of the lending officer and his or her insight when appraising the borrower's ability and willingness to repay. It is similar to the evaluation of a mortgage loan or a business loan. In addition the applicant's character and use of funds, the primary source of repayment and secondary or collateral source of repayment are also evaluated. In the judgmental method of credit analysis, the character can be evaluated from the applicant's credit history and the degree of dependability demonstrated through length and consistency of employment, length and type of residency, and other factors. A loan officer must be as objective as possible without applying subjective values or personal biases. The applicant's income is almost always the primary source of repayment of consumer loans. Income, therefore, must be adequate in relation to the borrower's debt and other financial obligations. Secondary sources of repayment should also be evaluated, and the present and probable future value of the collateral offered must be assessed.

Empirical Credit Analysis. Empirical credit scoring assigns points values to various applicant characteristics. Points are then added to award the applicant a numerical score, which is then compared to a predetermined accept/reject score. Credit is automatically granted to applicants with scores which equal or exceed the benchmark score. Credit is denied to those who are below that level.

An example of a credit scoring system is provided in Table 6–5. Note that each applicant characteristic used in the scoring system is weighted so that any one characteristic can have no more influence than another. Under ECOA such systems cannot use race, color, religion, national origin, or immigration status. Unlike the judgmental systems, empirical systems under ECOA can consider age but only as a positive factor. The regulation requires that the scoring system be based on data from an appropriate sample of applicants. It also requires that the system separate creditworthiness from non-creditworthiness in a statistically significant rate, and that it be periodically reevaluated as to the ability to predict good versus bad loans.

The proclaimed "pure" objectivity of credit scoring systems is appealing. However, such systems require highly sophisticated statistical tools which make it expensive to derive and to revalidate periodically. The objective of credit scoring is to predict from applicant characteristics whether a borrower is creditworthy or not. Multiple regression analysis or multiple discriminate analysis (MDA) determine the statistical importance of each characteristic and how that characteristic can be combined with others to distinguish bad from good loans. An illustration of a credit scoring system is presented in Figure 6–3. The figure shows the three-dimensional diagram of a simple credit scoring system with only two applicant characteristics: time with present employer on the Y axis, and income on the X axis. In reality, credit scoring systems use as many as 10 to 15 characteristics. They cannot be plotted as easily because each characteristic requires its own dimensions. The figure

Table 6–5: Sample Credit Scoring System Characteristics and Weights

		Points			Points
1	Own or rent principal residence			e. Loan only	10
	a. Owns/buying	40		f. None given	10
	b. Rents	8		g. No answer	10
	c. No answer	8	6.	Major credit card/dept. store	
	d. Other	25		a. Major CC(s) and department	
2.	Time at present address			store(s)	40
	a. Under 6 months	12		b. Major CC(s) only	40
	b. 6 months – 2 years	15		c. Department store(s) only	30
	c. 2 years – 6½ years	22		d. None	10
	d. Over 6½ years	35	7.	Finance company reference	
	e. No answer	12		a. One	15
3.	Time with present employer			b. Two or more	10
	a. Under 1½ years	12		c. None	5
	b. 1½ y – 3 years	15		d. No answer	10
	c. 3 years – 5½ years	25	8.	Income	
	d. Over 5½ years	48		a. $0 – 10,000	5
	e. Retired	48		b. $10,000 – 15,000	15
	f. Unemployed with alimony/			c. $15,000 – 30,000	30
	child support/public assistance	25		d. Over $30,000	50
	g. Homemaker	25	9.	Monthly payments	
	h. Unemployed—no public			a. $0 – $100	35
	assistance	12		b. $100 – 300	25
	i. No answer	12		c. Over $300	10
4.	Applicant's age			d. No payments	45
	a. Under 45 years	4		e. No answer	10
	b. 45 years or older	20	10.	Derogatory ratings	
	c. No answer	4		a. No investigation	0
5.	Banking reference			b. No record	0
	a. Checking and savings	60		c. Two or more derogatory	–20
	b. Checking	40		d. One derogatory	0
	c. Savings	40		e. All positive ratings	15
	d. Loan and checking and/or				
	savings	30			

Reprinted from Paul E. Green and Donald S. Tull, *Research for Marketing Decisions.* Englewood Cliffs, New Jersey: Prentice-Hall, 1970. Reprinted with permission.

Figure 6–3: Illustration of a Scoring System

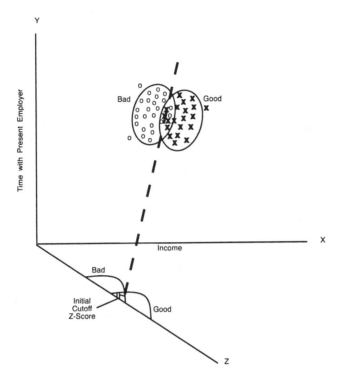

Adapted from Paul E. Green and Donald S. Tull, *Research for Marketing Decisions*. Englewood Cliffs, New Jersey, Prentice Hall, 1970

presents a simplified, two-dimensional credit saving system, with circles designated "bad" and Xs designated "good." The boundaries of each group are drawn to enclose a specific proportion of related points, such as 98 percent. Notice that the boundary enclosing 98 percent of one group also encloses a small proportion of the other group.

Now we draw a straight line through the points at which the group's boundaries intersect and project the line to the Z axis. This is the line condensed into the Z score which best separates the "bads" from the "goods." Also, the bad and good group points themselves are projected into the Z axis where they form frequency distribution for their Z scores. These distributions overlap, indicating the existence of a few bad borrowers among the good borrowers group and a few good borrowers in the bad borrowers group.

The cutoff Z score can be adjusted toward the origin in figure X below to liberalize credit granting. This adjustment would reduce the elimination of good borrowers but would also increase acceptance of bad borrowers. Adjusting further away from the origin would reduce the acceptance of bad borrowers and also eliminate more good borrowers. The credit scoring system illustrated in the figure combines the two characteristic profiles of good and bad borrowers into simple numbers. The line projected to the Z axis that best discriminates between good and bad borrowers implicitly assigns uniquely to each of the two characteristics.

Statistically derived credit scoring systems have two technical flaws that are commonly cited. First, the borrower's data used are historical and may be obsolete in detecting current predictors of creditworthiness. Second, the data consists of only those loan applications that have been accepted and does not consider applications that have been rejected. There is no actual record of creditworthiness of rejected applicants.

Both systems, judgmental and empirical, have their benefits. In comparing them, one should consider their ability to predict the creditworthiness of the applicant. If creditworthiness is successfully predicted, the thrift is protected against major losses and is assured of a predictable flow of payments. However, there are other factors to consider in this comparison, such as management's control over the process of granting credit. Control factors such as consistency and objectivity are important to the lender's reputation and to its obligation to comply with laws and regulations.

Both systems could use the same applicant characteristics. However, credit scoring assigns weight to each characteristic and reflects a hierarchy of their significance. In other words, the system consistently weighs each characteristic according to its statistical importance in relation to other characteristics. Judgmental systems are subject to variation of the hierarchy of significance. In addition, they may consider certain intangible factors that cannot be quantified, while credit scoring considers only quantifiable characteristics as well as those that have been associated historically with creditworthiness. Credit scoring can also consider a multitude of creditworthiness characteristics simultaneously, whereas judgmental systems are incapable of doing so due to the limitations of our human mental processes.

Overall, credit scoring is effective in processing large volumes while meeting regulatory requirements and simultaneously considering multiple variables. It cannot, however, take into account present and future changes in economic conditions, or the character of the borrower which could be incorporated by an

Table 6-6: Comparison of the Empirical and Judgmental Credit Evaluation Systems

EMPIRICAL	JUDGMENTAL
Endures objectivity	Involves objectively
Simultaneously considers multiple variables	Sequentially considers multiple variables
Efficient	Incorporates qualitative variable
Fast	More costly
Requires expertise to install	More time consuming
	Leverages existing fixed cost
Recommendation: apply to all loan applications	Recommendation: apply to borderline cases

experienced loan officer. In practice, many banks use a combination of judgmental and credit scoring systems. The credit scoring system readily isolates the clearly creditworthy and clearly non-creditworthy applicants. Those that fall in the grey zone are evaluated by a judgmental method (see Table 6-4).

6. Price and Structure the Credit

The analysis conducted and information gathered should serve as a basis for the pricing and credit-structuring decision. For example, if the analysis yields a high credit rating, the price will be lower, to reflect the risk-return relationship. If, on the other hand, the analysis indicates a marginally creditworthy customer, the interest rate charged would be high, and collateral may be needed in order to grant the loan.

The Role of Technology

Consumer lending can become more profitable through the use of technology. The trend toward automation could help cut costs and achieve more efficient and personal customer service.

Artificial intelligence in expert systems has many applications in the consumer lending business. An expert system is a form of artificial intelligence where software is programmed to behave like an expert in a particular field or function. It is expected to use reasoning, judgment, and problem solving strategies that are similar to humans. A banking expert system may contain thousands of rules that are linked together rationally to make the desired connection between a thorny problem and the optimal solution.

The primary goal of an expert system is to create a consistent, thorough, and objective decision-making resource that can be of value bank wide, regardless of the skills of any particular user. Expert systems have no hidden agendas and no corporate politics. They don't retire and can't be hired away by the competition, thereby preserving resident expertise and making it widely available to all when it is required, regardless of geographic location.

Expert systems are used to improve customer service and enhance staff professionalism. In the consumer lending area, expert systems have been devised to improve decision making and turnaround time. Arthur Andersen & Company has developed a PC-based mortgage analyzer. That system advises and learns from lending officers. It processes, evaluates, and draws preliminary conclusions from more than 200 data elements which are typically included in any loan package. The system then asks the loan officer questions that require subjective input. Finally, the officer analyzes the system's loan evaluation report and makes the decision whether or not to approve the loan. That decision is then documented into the system. This way the system continues to learn from the officers ongoing loan application loan decisions.

In addition to being based on Fannie Mae, Freddie Mac, and VA/FHA underwriting guidelines, the system incorporates the bank's specific lending policies and expert officers' rules of thumb. It is also compatible with a variety of mainframe environments. There are other applications to such systems, including credit cards and limit approval.

Expert systems have been developed for mortgages, commercial, and consumer loans. There has also been considerable research in the area of consumer credit scoring. Classical models incorporated several variables, including occupation, industry in which employed stability of employment, stability of residence, credit record, number of dependents and primary monthly income.

As one is considering entering the complex world of automation and expert systems, the first rule of thumb is the most difficult to enforce: go slowly. This is not to suggest that a thrift should walk away from a market opportunity but rather that it should make the investment today to ensure that the mix of technology and management is in place before a business strategy is launched. Staffing, training, retention, architecture; all the basic questions have to be addressed before a change is made—not after.

In applying technology, one should recognize that expert systems are complex and ever evolving. Perhaps, the best approach to utilizing technology in consumer lending is to start small, with a low profile, low risk, non-critical application. The system should be created to be easy to modify when requirements or new regulations dictate. The system evolves over time in accordance with technological advances, industry changes and the thrift's strategic goals. A thrift should test the assumptions, including management's assumptions about the role and place of expert systems within the institution's information systems, prior to installation. Don't believe everything you hear or read; rather, armed with the facts and encouraged by other successes and with the belief that technology can further strengthen your thrift's performance and profits, launch your own investigation of the ways technology can enhance your business, and draw your own conclusions.

The Risks of Consumer Lending

Consumer lending can be a panacea. It can, however, also be a nightmare. Both indirect lending through automobile dealers and unsecured consumer lending can be appropriate assets if management is committed to the discipline and expense necessary to assess and control risks. These are highly competitive fields but they can produce volume and profit.

With indirect lending, the essential risk assessment feature is verification of actual cash down payment by the buyer and employment data. The application that the bank receives does not come from the borrower rather from dealer's financing insurance manager, and while the overwhelming majority of these managers are honest they are all under pressure to finance sales. That pressure accelerates during recessionary periods. Approaching direct lending first is a prudent move.

Unsecured consumer lending is another area that can produce good results if time and money are invested to assess the true risks associated with the assets. Far too many lenders, however, underwrite consumer lines at inception and rely on payment history to be a precursor of trouble. Unfortunately, slow pay has become a poor warning sign, given the onslaught of bankruptcies in recent years. Should you elect to introduce unsecured consumer lines of credit or credit card lending, you must invest money and man power to review the credit bureau report at least annually prior to the renewal date, and preferably more frequently than that. The review must be frequent if any weakness has surfaced. If the credit bureau report shows a significant amount of revolving debt, even if present payments are being met, exiting should be considered. Let another bank extend credit to those bankruptcies awaiting to happen.

Training

Consumer lending training is essential to success and to making good loans. Consumer lending classes generally work best when enrollment is kept to 15 or 20 students. Initial credit training can be completed in less than two weeks if ongoing training is planned in the banker's future career path. The best teachers are those who have experienced retail and consumer lending firsthand. The course should teach students how to take loan applications, gather credit information, and complete and analyze financial statements. It should also address criteria for making credit decisions, loan documentation procedure, and ways to cope with potential collection problems. Credit investigation, collateral usage, structuring of the loan, and interest rate considerations are also integral parts of understanding consumer lending.

The credit underwriting criteria should include, at minimum, eight factors:

◆ Job stability

◆ Residence stability

◆ Loan amount

◆ Loan purpose

◆ Credit history

◆ Disposable income relative to aggregate current debt obligations

◆ Net worth

◆ Collateral

All the factors must be examined even if only one or two of them seem to argue convincingly for or against a loan. Just because someone has been in the same job twelve years and nets $4,500 per paycheck does not mean he can pay back every creditor. His other obligations may be much larger relative to his income. Likewise, a newly arrived person in the city, new on a job, may represent an excellent credit risk if this was a solid career move representing progress, and if his other obligations are a lot smaller relative to his income.

Lenders cannot afford to take shortcuts or leap to conclusions. Consequently, credit trainers should emphasize obtaining complete information as a critical part of the decision making process. Role playing can be used to help students master the art of gathering the necessary information. It is also helpful to assign students to present actual loan situations which call upon the student to go beyond the raw numbers and make the actual credit decision.

Credit Card Finance

Credit card loans have been the fastest growing of all consumer lending areas in recent years. They first became popular nearly twenty-five years ago. At that time, many local banks issued their own cards and recruited local merchants who agreed to accept the card from customers. Participating merchants presented the bank with vouchers signed by the credit card using customers on a daily basis. Their bank accounts then received immediate credit less the bank's discount.

That system, although beneficial to all three parties, had some serious drawbacks. A card's usefulness was restricted to those participating merchants and the bank's market area, and the competition among banks forced merchants to choose one plan to the exclusion of another. In the late 1960s, two national card plans emerged—Visa and MasterCard. Today, the issuing bank extends revolving credit to card holders and collects merchant fees to compensate for the costs it incurs associated with the operating systems.

An important feature of the national card system is the nationwide computer credit record maintained on card users. Merchants can call into their card issuing bank for credit verification on card users. The issuing bank acts as the national file to determine whether the proposed purchase would put the card user over his or her credit limit. By 1986 there were 72 million bank card holders in the United States and 148 million worldwide. During 1984, Visa alone had $70 billion worth of purchases charged on its cards. The Visa and MasterCard credit cards are not only convenient for consumer credit, but they also present a convenient alternative payment form.

Credit Card Pricing

Merchant discount fees generally range from 1 percent to 6 percent with high volume merchants paying lower discounts. The profitability of the business, however, relates much more to the usage of credit by the customer. Many states have usury laws that govern what banks can charge consumers for using their credit cards. Even today, there is debate whether banks can change annual fees and late charges outside of their home state. Some states, such as South Dakota, have no usury ceiling and therefore attract major credit card issuers. Bank credit card pricing is vulnerable to criticism as onerous and may be reregulated following a period of liberalization in the late 1980s.

Critical Success Factors

In order to be successful in the consumer lending business, several elements must be in place:

Management Commitment to the Business

Top management must lend its support to the business. It it important to hire professionals who know and understand consumer banking and give them the necessary support. The ideal team would include individuals with highly diverse backgrounds and expertise in marketing, direct sales, operations, risk management, financial control, and treasury operations.

Well-Defined Products

Any product chosen should be easily serviced and potentially profitable. Considerable time and effort must go into the planning with every consumer product, because once it is defined, loans could then be booked and administered with minimum labor intensity. The terms and conditions to each consumer loan product, whether it is a used car loan, installment loan, or a credit card, must all be clearly spelled out. These terms include the pricing, the terms of the loan, the dollar advance, payment penalties, the credit underwriting criteria, the method of screening and scoring, verification, and so on.

All items should be well defined in advance. It is during the planning period that the thrift needs to decide whether it can meet the intense competition and the high risk and reward of certain consumer businesses such as the credit card business. The questions that should be asked include issues such as: "Should our thrift offer credit cards, pre-approved, on local, regional, or on a nationwide basis, or should we just stick to offering the more familiar first and possibly second mortgages within our own territory?" There is a vast difference in the risk/reward tradeoff between these two alternatives, and the level of investment and management when needed to successfully implement either one.

Actuarial Management and Feedback

With the exception of first mortgages, consumer loan portfolios involve a certain measure of actuarial management. The scoring systems enable managers to compute the odds that certain events will take place. For example, application scoring allows lenders to estimate the degree of risk that should be attributed to first-time borrowers. Other scoring systems predict the usage of their response rate of potential customers. Behavior scoring systems predict the actions of people already booked, allowing lenders to lengthen or deepen the relationship with good customers and limit it with bad ones.

Management should also understand the limitations of credit scoring. Scoring can arrange the portfolio by risk or response rate, profitability, and by the odds of going bankrupt, among other factors. It can also feed management with the information for testing every type of alternative strategy, but scoring cannot predict which individual loan will go sour. Furthermore, scoring systems take time to install, are expensive, require strong system support, and must be incorporated into the business before the full benefits can be derived.

Economies of Scale

The large volume of loans involved in consumer lending requires that management understands and controls costs in great detail. Key cost elements include the following:

◆ The cost of acquiring customers, including marketing and advertising costs and the cost of analyzing accounts reviewed, but not lent to.

◆ Recurring servicing costs such as monthly processing, customer service, and maintenance expense.

◆ Collections expense which vary directly with the delinquencies levels of the portfolio.

◆ Overhead and other administrative expense.

All these cost-related functions are best handled with centralized controls and the business adapted to consider the unique elements of consumer lending. For example, customers prefer to be called in the evening. Sometimes out-of-state applications must be screened quickly and accurately and the results phoned back to the dealer waiting for the fastest answer. Collectors must be supported with the latest power dialing equipment. Consumer lending, therefore, is profitable, but requires close monitoring of costs and a cultural change.

Funding

Cost of funds is an integral ingredient of the profitability of the loan which really is a major determinant of the cost. Three alternatives are available to the thrifts' treasurer:

1. *Fund everything on a short-term basis.* This would work in a declining environment and may still function in a stable one, but may lose the bank in a rising rate environment.

2. *Match funds on a term basis to the loan.* This very conservative approach may not maximize profits, but minimizes risks.

3. *Sell and securitize as many assets as possible from the secondary market.* This tactic gets the asset off the books so that interest rate management becomes someone else's problem.

Treasurers may use any combination of the above alternatives but explicit policies must be established as to the funding programs for consumer loans.

7

*Mortgage Banking: Leveraging the Branch and Origination Network**

There are quite a few thrifts which remained successful through difficult times by sticking to their knitting: the traditional business of mortgage origination. These thrifts maintained profitability by being conservative. They kept costs to a minimum, used highly conservative underwriting criteria, and developed strong relationships with their depository customers. For those thrifts which are structured to provide exactly what their customer base requires, sticking to what they have done well in the past may prove successful in the future. At the same time, competition for mortgage customers is increasing, and many thrifts may have to change to meet new challenges. Commercial banks and insurance companies are competing harder than ever for mortgage dollars since residential mortgages are regarded as relatively safe loans and real estate investments in today's market.

The thrift industry's historical domination of the mortgage market has been threatened by the many changes which occurred in the 1980s with regional economic downturns, mismanagement, and the adverse effects of deregulation. Now a

*The author wishes to thank Amy Glick for her valuable contribution to this chapter.

restructured residential real estate industry has emerged. There are new players in the mortgage markets, with much more finely segmented business lines. There is also an increasingly efficient and sophisticated secondary mortgage market. Mortgages are becoming more of a commodity, and mortgage banking and yields are becoming more competitive. Given these new conditions, thrifts should consider strategies to increase revenues through the secondary mortgage market. Diversifying to provide new or complementary sources of revenues will be the solution for the long-term growth and survival of many thrift institutions.

Mortgage banking offers one such diversification solution, building on the perceived strength of many thrifts in mortgage origination. The business as it is discussed here has three main components: origination, secondary market sales, and servicing.

Mortgage origination as used here refers to both mortgages originated in the institution's own name and mortgages which thrifts originate as correspondents to larger institutions.

Secondary market sales involve exchanging the income stream from the loan for a front-end payment, either by selling the whole loans themselves or as securitized instruments.

Servicing may be performed for loans generated by the originating thrift itself, by others, or both.

Following an examination of the benefits of entry into the secondary mortgage market, we will discuss thrifts' competitive advantages, market attractiveness, and critical success factors. Finally, mortgage banking trends for the 1990s and beyond will be discussed.

Benefits of Entry into the Secondary Mortgage Market

Entering the secondary mortgage market can be thought of as an extension of the thrift's product line which offers several benefits: fee income, off-balance sheet transactions, and increased capital and liquidity. All of these benefits increase current income without the burdens of long-term risk.

Fee Income

Fees are most commonly generated through mortgage origination, packaging the loans for sale, and servicing. In other words, each segment of the mortgage banking chain produces fee income for its participants. This fee income can either be reinvested or used to offset the pricing pressures on conventional mortgages as they become increasingly commoditized.

Thrifts can also generate fees in the mortgage banking business by buying or selling mortgage servicing rights. Buyers can benefit from an increase in fee income from servicing operations, and sellers can improve earnings by booking the sales gain on an off-balance-sheet asset in the current accounting period, thereby realizing immediate profits. Thrifts should, however, avoid purchasing servicing at a price substantially above its economic value as the intangible assets created in the process weather the institution's perceived capital profits.

Valuation, then, is essential. The seller must be required to provide an accurate and complete package of information on the servicing rights being offered. This involves obtaining data on the servicing rights being sold, ensuring its accuracy, and computing critical financial information by type of loan and by type of servicing. Successful sales of servicing must be planned to allow ample time and resources to perform the necessary evaluations.

Capital Benefits

Thrifts remove loans from their balance sheets by selling them in the secondary markets. This process enables them to convert the mortgages' future cash flows into current income. It also increases capital (through realizing a gain) and liquidity (through the conversion of longer term assets into cash) while lowering their total assets (and therefore their capital requirements).

The liquid, deep secondary market in mortgages permits thrifts to originate mortgages while avoiding many significant costs: the associated capital and risk-based capital requirements, deposit insurance premiums on the funding of the assets, and interest rate risk-management related costs associated with the funding of a long-term asset. These savings may be converted into additional capital, which would otherwise need to be obtained through an equity issue and therefore be subject to the investors' return requirements and corporate income taxes. Use of the secondary mortgage market can also intensify the utilization (turnover) of available bank capital because, if it is not needed to fulfill reserve requirements, the income received from sale of a mortgage portfolio may be lent out again.

Liquidity

Improved liquidity management is another reason for entering the secondary mortgage market. Selling mortgages increases thrifts' liquidity because it generates current income, and because thrifts do not have to reserve for assets they do not carry on their balance sheets. A thrift can access investor markets through both loan and deposit sales. By conducting these sales continuously, a thrift can attempt to maximize the risk-adjusted yield on the total loan portfolio. This creates liquidity on both the asset and liability sides of the balance sheet. Thrifts which can master the knowledge and techniques of selling loans create, in effect, an extra liquidity reserve. They also gain additional flexibility in their liquidity management by being able to more easily manage both sides of the balance sheet.

Lower Credit Risk

Selling mortgages in the secondary market lowers thrifts' exposure to credit risk. Off-balance-sheet lending lowers default risk by allowing thrifts to diversify their loan portfolios. Many thrifts traditionally specialized in originating a single type of loan, such as mortgages. Many have portfolios which are geographically concentrated. By entering the secondary market, a thrift can sell those loans it considers undesirable to hold on its own balance sheet for credit or other reasons, and use the proceeds to diversify its loan portfolio by acquiring different types of loans.

Interest Rate Risk Management

Selling mortgages in the secondary market can also be used to lower a thrift's interest rate risk. It takes loans off the balance sheet and effectively changes the thrift's asset mix. While traditional forms of gap management are considered low-risk when interest rates are relatively stable, the use of the secondary mortgage market becomes especially important when interest rates are volatile or rising.

Traditional risk management techniques, such as duration gap analysis and maturity gap analysis, require detailed data on expected cash flows, interest rates, and maturities of the bank's assets and liabilities. This precise information is not always readily available, and it often requires making many assumptions. In contrast, the sale of mortgages in the secondary markets is a transaction which removes the risk from a balance sheet altogether. It involves no interest rate predictions; instead, it simply represents the trading of a series of future cash flows for one present payment. Once a loan sale or securitization is consummated, unlike traditional gap management, the thrift bears no future interest rate risk associated with that particular postage.

Origination and servicing can be viewed as hedges against each other. When market demand for mortgages is low, servicing income compensates for lower origination fees; and in strong origination markets, production growth serves as a hedge against prepayments.

Flexibility

Mortgage originators such as thrifts can take advantage of growth in the secondary markets. This secondary market gives thrifts the flexibility to hold a small portfolio on their balance sheets while using their established loan origination network and customer relationships to continue to generate income by producing additional loans which will then be sold in the secondary market.

While all these benefits improve the financial condition of thrifts, and should be considered strong incentives on their own to enter the secondary mortgage market, there is an additional consideration which supports the benefits of this business diversification: Survival. Many banks and non-banks have rushed in to fill the void in the mortgage origination market left by weak thrifts. The new non-bank market participants, such as insurance companies, retailers and brokers, are not subject to the tightened restrictions of the Financial Institutions Reform, Recovery and Enforcement Act of 1989 and to other depository institutions regulatory constraints. This intensifying pressure and increasingly competitive, restructured mortgage market puts further pressure on thrifts, the traditional mortgage providers.

Thrifts must build on their current strengths. Developing secondary market operations to improve profitability and lower risk is one important option to be considered in the context of future survival.

Competitive Advantages

As more and more financial institutions enter the various components of the mortgage business and competition intensifies, those thrifts which maintain their ability to generate a high volume of creditworthy mortgages are at a competitive advantage. Thrifts often have strong customer loyalty and market presence. They can continue to attract mortgage customers and differentiate themselves from other competitors in the marketplace through superior customer service and their understanding of local markets. Thrifts have two built-in competitive advantages in the mortgage banking market: their origination network is already in place, and most already have a strong reputation for customer service.

Origination can take place through the thrift's current network of mortgage loan officers, real estate broker relationships, and retail bank branches. Knowledge of the local marketplace and customer contact are important factors in attracting customers. These can be augmented by various tools. For example, some successful mortgage originators offer educational seminars as a service to both potential customers and realtors. It is beneficial for the thrift to offer potential customers a seminar, for example, on what it takes to obtain a mortgage. Education could bring in customers who were unaware that they were qualified to obtain mortgages. It also often produces better prepared loan applicants. Realtors can also benefit from information on the thrift's mortgage products and general underwriting standards. By providing services such as these on a consistent basis, a thrift can maintain contact with its two primary sources of loans, as well as establish the relationships and goodwill to generate further business. The continuing customer contact and service that thrifts supply to the community gives them a differential advantage in mortgage origination.

Market Attractiveness

Market Growth

Current statistics on the mortgage market and the industry segments participating in it are not always available. Recent information on the ten largest mortgage originators (Table 7–1) indicates that the total mortgage market has been growing in the past three years. That growth is expected to continue during the low interest environment despite recesstionary pressures.

The thrift industry's share of the mortgage market has been declining consistently. Commercial banks surpassed thrifts as the originators of most mortgages in 1989, and the gap has evidenced since that time (see Figures 7–1 and 7–2).

Profitability

The cost structures of the origination and servicing aspects of mortgage banking are fundamentally different. Profits in the mortgage banking industry are typically generated primarily through loan servicing rather than through origination activities.

Origination can be an unprofitable to marginally profitable activity, for the mortgage banker. Origination expenses are netted against fee income. Application fees are used to fund the cost of obtaining appraisals, credit reports, and other credit verification. In addition, due to complex pricing arrangements with correspondents, loan brokers, or other parties involved in some aspect of the transaction, the points received at loan closing may not all belong to the originating entity. The number of points received at closing is determined primarily by market forces,

Table 7-1: Top Ten Mortgage Originators
(in billion of dollars)

	1991	1990	1989
Norwest Corp.	13.22	12.30	12.30
Fleet/Norstar	11.20	11.90	11.10
Prudential Home	10.30	10.60	10.10
Citicorp Mortgage	10.00	10.10	8.70
Countrywide Funding	9.70	8.80	4.70
Bank of America	9.00	7.20	4.60
Home Savings of America	8.37	5.84	4.50
Great Western	7.50	4.52	4.40
Sears Mortgage	6.60	4.40	4.40
Chemical Mortgage	6.40	4.31	4.40
	92.69	79.97	59.20

Source: FNMA

rather than by the expense associated with originating a loan. As a result, origination costs are difficult to pass through to the customer, and fees may not cover all the expenses incurred.

The costs of origination are many. Thrifts often pay originators a commission of approximately 50 basis points for each loan that closes. This represents a substantial portion of total fee income. Salary costs are substantial given the need to maintain a permanent staff of processors, underwriters, closers, and administrators. Building overhead can also be substantial if a thrift maintains a branch network or does not have centralized or regionalized underwriting. Additional costs include communication, legal, and document preparation. Document preparation is, however, becoming more automated, and is increasingly being outsourced in efforts to ensure originators' compliance with regulations across state lines.

Competitive Profile

The economics of mortgage banking have changed over the past several years, just as the economics of the marketplace have changed. Mortgage banking has become a more complex segment of the financial services industry. The mortgage banker

Figure 7–1: Home Mortgages Held by Banks and Healthy Thrifts

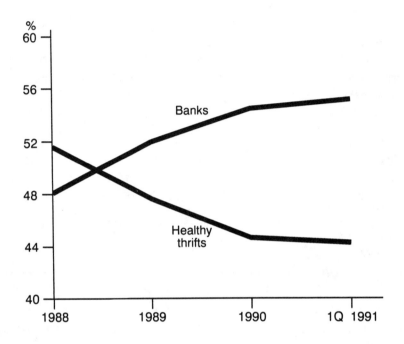

Source: W. C. Ferguson & Co., Office of Thrift Supervision, and Resolution Trust Corporation

must offer a wide array of mortgage products to borrowers whose preferences change from one loan type to another with shifts in the economy, interest rates, and their own expectations. For example, the market share of originations of fixed-rate loans fluctuates with interest rate cycles. In the past, as mortgage rates fell below 10 percent, fixed-rate mortgages dominated the market. Conversely, when interest rates rise, adjustable-rate mortgages become more popular. Issuing Adjustable Rate Mortgages (ARMs) has some benefits, including lowering interest rate risk over the life of the loan, and lowering credit risk for the first few years of a loan (since the payments are typically lower and easier for borrowers to meet). At the same time, when payments rise, credit risk increases.

Figure 7–2: Banks Are Increasing Market Share

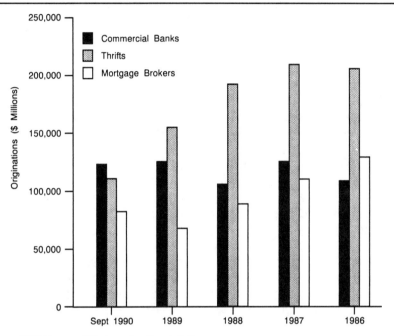

Source: HUD Survey of Mortgage Lending Activity

With each shift in the mortgage market, the mortgage banker's interest rate risk and credit risk positions change. The mortgage banker needs to continually monitor mortgage market conditions and take actions which will maintain target risk levels. Purchasing and selling mortgages in the secondary market is one technique of risk management which should be considered.

Since the development of the secondary market, mortgage banking has become inextricably linked to the capital markets.[1] The mortgage market has mirrored the volatility of the capital markets, and the spread between mortgage and Treasury yields has become narrower over the past twenty years as the market's efficiency increased and transactions became more standardized.[2]

---

1 Mike Devaney and Karen Pickerill, "The Integration of Mortgage and Capital Markets," *The Appraisal Journal,* Jan. 1990, pp. 109–113.

2 Devaney and Pickerill, "The Integration of Mortgage and Capital Markets."

The volatility of the secondary mortgage market induces many lenders to continue to offer significant front-end discounts on adjustable mortgages as a preferred more predictable risk management tool. This, coupled with the short-term orientation of the capital markets, makes fixed-rate loans less attractive to lenders. Borrowers are expected to pay compensating fees to the lenders due to these conditions. This is but one example of the impact of the secondary mortgage market on the primary origination market.

In addition, borrowers should experience difficulty in obtaining long-term loan commitments at a fixed rate without paying compensating fees; this is caused by the shorter term orientation of the capital markets.[3] In fact, because of the growth of the secondary market, mortgage origination criteria are increasingly dictated by the demands of the capital markets, as originators want to ensure their flexibility to enter the secondary markets in the future.

Both the globalization of the capital markets and the volatility of interest rates are risk factors which have made mortgage banking a more complex and difficult business to manage.

The globalization of capital markets introduced factors such as political risk, exchange rates, and trade balances into the process of determining interest rates. It has also attracted purchasers for secondary mortgages on a global scale. This has the benefit of widening the base of potential purchasers. At the same time, though, secondary mortgages must compete with investment alternatives around the world for their share of the global capital pool.

Interest rate volatility increases interest rate related risks for mortgage bankers. The spread between an institution's cost of funds and its interest revenues, or "pure" interest rate risk, is less predictable in a volatile interest rate environment. The basis for the mortgage bank's cost of funds and the basis it uses to determine the borrower's interest rate may be different. Even if the rates are determined by the same base, the mortgage bank may not be able to immediately pass through changes in its cost of funds to the borrower. A lender could then be stuck with a smaller than anticipated spread, and therefore lower earnings.

Interest rate volatility also increases the risks of mortgage prepayment, refinancing, pipeline risk (discussed later in the chapter) and credit problems. If rates rise, some borrowers will prepay their mortgages to avoid the high interest costs; if rates drop, borrowers often refinance their mortgages. Pipeline risk is also greater in a volatile rate environment, since wide interest rate swings which might occur

---

3   Devaney and Pickerill, "The Integration of Mortgage and Capital Markets."

while a loan is in the pipeline could eliminate the bank's profit spread or greatly increase the credit risk if payments increase sharply.

Credit problems can develop if rates increase substantially and borrowers cannot make their loan payments. These risks become more likely when interest rates are more volatile. These risks are also less predictable when interest rates are volatile. It is more difficult to properly price loans to compensate for these risks in an unpredictable, volatile interest rate environment. The net result is that primary mortgage lenders charge borrowers more because of the increased risk they must bear and the uncertainty associated with it, and the mortgages are regarded as riskier investments by potential secondary market purchasers.

These new conditions have created an environment where much greater resources are necessary to compete effectively. These resources range from financial modeling and interest rate forecasting to comprehensive computer systems and higher capital requirements. It is now more difficult for the smaller, independent firms to effectively compete. As a result, many of the medium and larger mortgage banks have become subsidiaries of larger institutions.

This consolidation trend is ongoing, and it remains a major characteristic of the secondary mortgage business today. As the secondary markets have grown in importance, participants in mortgage banking have changed to reflect the integration of mortgage banking with the capital markets. Many new financial and non-financial institution players have entered the market. The composition of the players in the mortgage banking industry has changed as loan sales in the secondary market have shifted from being an unusual occurrence to being an integral part of depository institutions' balance sheet management.

Thrifts have also been selling their mortgages in the secondary markets in order to maintain a competitive position in residential mortgage origination as well as to overcome the financial difficulties of the 1980s. The ability to sell mortgages in the secondary markets allows thrifts to remain active in mortgage origination, even when the market does not meet their own portfolio investment criteria or where their capital position precludes further growth and leverage. The secondary market is also useful as a tool for thrifts in managing their interest rate exposure and asset/liability mix.

Securities dealers have a strong role in mortgage banking due to the importance of mortgage securities in the secondary market. Investment bankers are playing an increasing role in facilitating whole loan trading, portfolio restructuring transactions, and the purchase and sale of loan servicing rights. They function as intermediaries who often expedite information exchange and consummate transactions between the primary and secondary mortgage markets.

Commercial banks and bank holding companies use mortgage banking subsidiaries as a way to provide their customers with additional products and broaden the range of financial services they can offer consumers. These mortgage banking subsidiaries often benefit from the credit facilities offered by their parent commercial banks.

Non-financial corporations and holding companies are also building large mortgage banking operations. These entrants have been driven by their perception that economies of scale produce profits, and by the availability of resources to put national loan origination networks in place.

Life insurance companies have also become players, generally using mortgage banking subsidiaries as their sources of origination for residential loans.

Critical Mass/Economies of Scale

The concentration of players in the mortgage market is due to several factors including the shrinkage of the thrifts industry, the growth in marketing expertise, increased efficiencies in loan originations, and the commoditization of mortgages. The economies of scale necessary for profitability are driving the consolidation in mortgage servicing operations.

Over the past several years, the size of the major firms has increased dramatically in terms of both loan production volume and the size of the portfolios serviced. Annual loan originations of between $1 billion and $10 billion are common, and so are servicing portfolios of more than $10 billion.

The securities markets have influenced the drive for higher volumes of loan originations. With higher volumes, formation of collateral pools for mortgage-backed securities is quicker and less risky, making it easier and more cost effective to use Wall Street delivery mechanisms and to provide more control over risk exposure. Higher volumes also have pricing advantages in the securities markets.

Thrifts which generate smaller loan volumes often hold loans until a larger, more marketable critical mass has accumulated. The increased competition for a share of the origination market has shrunk profit margins, leaving less room to negotiate on the loan sales side of the business. This gives originators even more incentive to take advantage of any economies of scale which might exist.

It appears such economics are not present in a meaningful way on the origination side. Higher production volume does not significantly lower the per loan cost of origination. Figures from the Mortgage Bankers Association of America indicate no correlation between higher production volume and lower costs.

For mortgage bankers, loan originations have traditionally operated at a loss. The loss is tolerated and justified by the industry as the necessary cost of building the loan servicing portfolio. Traditionally, mortgage bankers have viewed the servicing portfolio as their primary asset and source of steady income. That view has been reinforced by the emergence of an active market in the purchase and sale of loan servicing rights which has added liquidity to the servicing portfolio. Many mortgage bankers purchase and sell servicing rights, depending on their working capital requirements.

Many thrift executives would disagree with the characterization of mortgage origination as unprofitable since they have generated substantial profits through their own mortgage origination operations for many years. The traditional thrift has originated and held mortgages for their own portfolio for many decades, and has done so successfully and profitably. However, as a component of the mortgage banking business, originations are not always the most profitable part of the equation.

While there may be some economies of scale in selling larger blocks of loan servicing, the market has no minimum required amounts. At the same time, since servicing rights are sometimes sold in conjunction with securitization, the economies of scale from the securities market (i.e., larger volume blocks sell at lower per unit costs) may spill over into the loan servicing area. Therefore, thrifts which generate a small volume of loans for servicing sales may opt to accumulate the volume and sell the servicing rights when the volume reaches a more marketable level. This would enable thrifts to take advantage of the better pricing offered by the public markets as compared to private investors.

Loan servicing operations, unlike loan production, do benefit from economies of scale. Operating a loan servicing department requires minimum levels of fixed costs to conduct servicing activities, primarily in facilities and data processing resources, and to a lesser extent in personnel. These minimum levels can also, within limits, accommodate larger volumes without directly proportional increases in costs.

These economies of scale only produce cost efficiencies up to a certain point. Per loan costs decline substantially up to $1 billion in servicing, but above that, marginal cost improvements are negligible. Increasing servicing portfolio size can, in fact, cause diminishing returns if the portfolio becomes so diversified in terms of products or geographic dispersion that servicing it becomes inefficient. Delinquency and foreclosure rates as well as adequacy of the systems' support have more impact on costs than the sheer number of loans serviced. In conclusion, loan servicing can benefit from economies of scale, but the efficiencies are limited.

Diversity of Products—One for Every Risk Profile

A relatively new, but central, characteristic of the mortgage banking industry today is the wide range of choices available to mortgage bankers. In addition to numerous loan products, there are many options and alternatives to consider in loan production, secondary marketing, and loan servicing.

Choosing which loan products to offer may be determined primarily by the marketplace. However, in addition to consumer demands, the requirements of the secondary mortgage market are also a consideration. Further, the institution must consider whether it intends to hold the loans originated for its own portfolio, and, if so, whether these loans will meet its own quality and return requirements.

Going beyond the choice of products, a mortgage banking operation can also choose the market segment in which it will participate. With the current specialization and segmentation of the functions in the industry, mortgage bankers can participate in one or any combination of origination, sales, and servicing. The ability to choose among such a wide variety of options offers management the opportunity to select and implement strategies which will be most appropriate and profitable for their institution.

This, of course, means that strategic planning is critical to the success of mortgage banking operations. It requires understanding of the economics as well as the long-term strategic implications of these choices in each functional area and as a combination. The following section discusses some of the factors which are critical to success in mortgage banking. Considering these factors is important in developing the right positioning for your institution in the mortgage banking market.

Critical Success Factors

Although competitive pricing is an ongoing necessity, it is not the only key to long-term success. The leaders in the mortgage banking business will continue to lower costs while improving products and services. Success in mortgage origination and servicing will be determined by a combination of a solid understanding of the fundamental economics of the business and the thrift's ability to differentiate its products and services by providing the features and benefits which customers desire.

Choosing a Strategic Direction

Choosing the appropriate strategic direction for a thrift's mortgage banking business, and considering entry possibilities are the first critical elements in success.

There is no one correct approach. Rather, management should take into account the thrift's existing financial and operational structure, competitive position, and its size and access to capital. A thrift must assess its strengths and weaknesses, as well as define the objectives it wants to achieve through entry into the secondary market in the short and long term, before attempting to select the right applications: origination, sales, servicing, or a combination of the three.

Whether the thrift chooses to provide service in only one or all portions of the mortgage cycle, loan liquidation should be part of a thrift's overall strategy. Loan product managers should view investors in the secondary market, the purchasers of the mortgage packages/pools, as being the end of the origination cycle. Loans should then be structured so that they can easily be sold or participated to the capital markets. The thrift will benefit from enhanced funds' flexibility, responsiveness to borrowers, and greater market efficiency through matching capital users with capital sources.

Deciding which area of mortgage lending to target depends to a large degree on the institution's size. With the trend toward consolidation, economies of scale are a reality of the competitive marketplace. As the trend continues, it will be increasingly difficult for smaller thrifts to compete unless they find ways to partake in the cost advantages of larger-scale operations. Although economies of scale are a factor in the economic success of a mortgage banking operation, medium-sized thrifts can be profitable full-service mortgage providers if they continue to focus on efficient productivity.

Since the marginal cost of servicing per loan drops dramatically as portfolio size increases, servicing portfolios of less than 15,000 loans is not cost efficient enough to be competitive. Smaller thrifts should look to a niche strategy to succeed. Correspondent lending is one niche where smaller thrifts can use their local market loan origination network to their advantage. Another potential strategy for smaller thrifts is to consider selling the servicing rights to their portfolio to larger institutions, or pool trust assets with other similar site peers.

As a correspondent lender, a thrift establishes a relationship with another financial institution which wants to hold or sell mortgages originated by the thrift. The thrift originates the transaction but does not carry the loan on its own balance sheet. Instead, the loans are booked on the buyer's balance sheet, and the thrift receives a fee for providing the origination service.

The thrift must originate within underwriting guidelines specified or approved by the purchasing institution, and it often must guarantee a minimum volume of originations as part of the correspondent agreement. The thrift which acts as a correspondent, then, is able to capitalize on its origination network without the burden of maintaining the mortgage banking intrastructure, including warehouse lines of credit, finding buyers in the secondary markets, or holding the loans in its own portfolio. At the same time, profitability is limited to one source and is dependent on the strength of the origination market.

A thrift which sells the servicing rights to its portfolio gains the upfront fees for the servicing without the burden of the overhead for a loan servicing operation. This thrift would have two sources of income from its mortgage banking operation: origination fees and servicing rights. It would, however, still hold the loans it originated on its balance sheet.

Origination Efficiencies

As discussed above, one advantage thrifts have in the origination function is their network of current relationships and their reputation in the marketplace. Another is their staff, which can be trained to originate and sell mortgages in addition to other responsibilities. Finally, improved automation can make origination more efficient.

Mortgage origination is an integral part of thrifts' traditional business strategy. Thrifts should keep in mind the basic formula for success in mortgage origination: high productivity, high marketability, and low unit costs. Thrifts should consciously choose the market segment, product mix, and delivery systems which will be most profitable or maximize other company objectives such as solidifying customer relationships.

While considering the thrift's current strengths is important, it is even more important to focus on customer needs and how to meet them. Both primary and secondary customer needs are important factors in successful mortgage marketing. The commitment to design products and delivery systems to satisfy primary customer needs in terms of product features, pricing structures, decision turnaround time, convenience, and personalized service is key to success.

Thrifts, as mortgage bankers, have the options of originating mortgages themselves, acquiring loans, or both. The choice is dictated, in part, by the size of the institution, since some small originators may not have a line of credit large enough to finance mortgage closings and warehouse the loans prior to sale. At the same time, leveraging an origination network is one of the major competitive advantages thrifts have as mortgage bankers. One option for small thrifts is to act as correspondent lenders by selling other lenders' mortgage products (i.e., closing mortgages funded by other institutions). This, in effect, gives the small thrift access to other banks' warehouse lines of credit, while expanding its own origination network.

Larger thrifts may be able to own the full range of origination activities, including processing and underwriting, provided that their servicing operations are profitable. They, too, may choose to augment their origination capabilities with loans purchased through correspondents. The purchase price and fee structure of loan acquisitions reflect the extent of the services performed by the correspondent. These may range from simply taking borrower applications to performing all loan processing functions through underwriting and closing.

Given the high costs of maintaining an origination network, successful originators need to focus on efficiency and leveraging the network through cross selling other related fee income generating products. Opportunities to improve productivity can be found in streamlining workflows and centralizing processing. Monitoring of productivity and quality is more effective within a central location where work processes can be segregated and standardized, and specialization by function can be achieved.

Most mortgages today are originated either through bank and thrift branches or through loan production offices. In any branch structure, branch managers or experienced loan officers handle walk-in business. They manage the origination from completing the loan application to preparing and ordering the documentation required for credit files. This enables them to use their existing facilities and customer base to generate new business. Leverage will be achieved only if the branch officers are not overburdened with consumer loan and administrative responsibilities.

Loan production offices allow dedicated officers to focus on mortgage origination, and they have been found to generate 33 percent higher unit volume, on average, than multi-functional officers based in branches.[4] Successful mortgage originators understand how to build and maintain referral networks. Their compensation structure also provides incentives to produce. Most dedicated loan production officers are paid on a commission basis rather than the salary and bonus system used for branch based originators. The commission structure not only provides incentives to employees but it also changes compensation from a fixed to a variable cost, thus lowering overhead.

Laptop computers are enabling mortgage originators to operate away from the sales office, thereby further reducing overhead, increasing productivity and improving customer service. The laptop enables the originator to prequalify applicants quickly and easily, allowing the loan officer to enter the application information directly into the system. This helps the borrower find out very quickly whether their loan will be approved. One future trend involves originators working out of

---

4   Waino Pihl, Jeanne Stewart, and Michael Wambay, "Mortgage Originations Apply Just-in-Time Principles to Strengthen Performance," *Bank Management,* June, 1991, p. 22.

their homes and conducting business wherever customer convenience and receptivity are maximized.

Phone sites are another growing loan delivery channel. Central phone sites have been found to be 25 percent more productive on a unit volume basis than loan production offices, and 66 percent more productive than branches. Turnaround time has also been found to be more efficient, averaging 27 days for both branches and loan production offices, but only 18 days for central phone sites.[5]

Centralizing processing operations, for instance, allows for increased efficiencies through processor specialization, better work load balancing, and improved supervision and training. Depending on the composition of the loan portfolio, processors can specialize by type of loan or by task. This segregation of duties creates more efficient workers. The cost of overhead per loan declines as the number of units processed per person increases. Work loads can be better balanced when all processors are in a central location. Supervision is tighter, and training is improved because employees can learn from others in the department in addition to formal training sessions.

Technology can also be used to enhance centralization efficiencies, but if not appropriate, can become a hindrance. An information system must be well thought out, integrated, and flexible enough to change with the competitive environment in order to improve efficiency. Computers can be used to standardize mortgage forms and reduce paper flows, thereby increasing processing efficiency. The data input tasks of processors can be reduced through use of computerized applications, automated credit report retrieval, and direct computer interface with appraisers. Automated document preparation and document tracking is also growing in popularity. Document tracking software provides information for improved management reporting on issues such as turnaround time and pipeline risk, and it can assist processors in building efficient work management procedures.

A good system will also help in tracking leads and in cross-selling efforts. With the ability to easily follow customer and product profitability trends, mortgage originators can identify their optimal product mix and most effective distribution channels, and then they can target their marketing efforts toward customer segments.

Information technology can also improve origination efficiency from a quality standpoint. Originators use technology to pre-qualify mortgage candidates, for instance through instantaneous information provided by credit reporting services. In addition, the originator can speed service and improve customer satisfaction by

---

5 Pihl, Stewart, and Wambay, "Mortgage Originations Apply Just-in-Time Principles to Strengthen Performance."

being able to select product alternatives and issue conditional commitments via computer.

Thrifts should use their knowledge of customer demographics and payment history to maximize origination productivity and cross sell additional products. Cross sales commonly involve other residential real estate loan products such as home equity loans or refinancings, related products such as credit life insurance, mortgage insurance and flood insurance, and banking products such as deposit accounts, consumer loans, or credit cards. Other services a thrift can offer through its existing distribution networks include insurance, income tax services, and bill consolidation loans. The delivery of multiple products and services not only generates revenues for the institution but also capitalizes on thrifts' reputation for customer service and fixed-cost base while strengthening customer loyalty.

Valuation of Servicing

Valuation of servicing portfolios is important in their purchase and sales as well as in limiting the capital tax imposed by FIRREA (The Financial Institutions Reform, Recovery, and Enforcement Act). The value of a mortgage servicing portfolio is the expected net present value of the future cash flow from all sources associated with the servicing portfolio. These cash flows are derived from the servicing activity income and the earnings on cash balances.

Servicing activity income is the difference between both the servicing fees and other fee income and the cost of servicing. Fees collected on the remaining balances of loans serviced range from .25 percent to .50 percent. Float also generates significant revenues since there is almost always a timing difference between receipt and disbursal of principal payments, interest payments, and escrow reserves. Late charges, assumptions, bad checks, copies of amortization schedules, and cross selling of related services generate fees as well. A further benefit, albeit one which does not necessarily create income, is the ability to manage the income statement through differential accounting treatment given to the sale and purchase of servicing portfolios.[6]

The main source of cash in the servicing portfolio is the escrow balance. Servicers collect tax, insurance, principal, and interest payments each month. These payments are held in an escrow account, and the tax and insurance payments are typically made once or twice a year. Earnings on these escrow balances

---

6 "FIRREA Tests Purchasers of Mortgage Servicing," *Savings Institutions,* Dec., 1988, pp. 72-73.

are the difference between the implicit earnings rate of free cash balances and any cost to pass through the earnings to the borrowers. In some states, lenders are required to pay borrowers interest at the passbook savings rate. In other states, there is no requirement to pay interest on escrow balances.

The second source of cash balances is the float on the principal and interest between the time payments are collected from the borrower and the time they are remitted to the holder of the mortgages. Some mortgage holders require that the lender pass through the monthly payment when it is due, whether the funds have been collected or not. In those cases, the servicer may need to advance funds to the mortgage holder for part of the month. This is, of course, a cost to the servicer.

One major difference between mortgage bankers and portfolio lenders is the way each accounts for the servicing activity. Mortgage bankers have a separate servicing cost center with a well-defined servicing fee as income. Portfolio lenders, in contrast, often view servicing as a loan administration cost, without a defined fee specifically attributable to servicing activities. The servicing fee is obscured because it is built into the interest rate charged to the borrower. For example, a mortgage banker collects a servicing fee to perform the servicing function, and this fee is subtracted from the interest paid on the loan. On a loan with an interest rate of $8\frac{1}{4}$ percent and an agreed upon servicing fee of $\frac{1}{4}$ percent, the investor would receive net interest of 8 percent. By establishing a separate cost center for servicing, thrifts can recognize the true value of the loan components and separate the value of the loan as a marketable security from the value of the servicing.

Costs involved in servicing are determined by the type of loans being serviced. The primary costs in servicing relate to personnel and data processing. Other costs include the lender's cost of advancing funds to the investor even when borrowers are late with payments, staff for accounting and record keeping when refinancing activity is heavy, reporting requirements for multiple investors, delinquency expenses, and potential interest payments on escrowed funds.

In addition, there is a one-time cost to put the loan into the servicing system. This "fixed" cost may include such variables as investor-related costs, transfer and register of mortgage-backed securities, or verification of data.

While no two servicing portfolios are alike, some general valuation guidelines may be helpful. Loans with low delinquency rates will have lower collection costs, and therefore, lower costs of servicing. Loan portfolios with many investors are usually more expensive to service than portfolios with few investors. Loans located in states which require interest payments on escrow accounts or in states which have longer foreclosure redemption periods will be less valuable than loans in states without those laws. Payment history also affects pricing. Seasoned mortgages which have payment histories of over one year are more valuable than portfolios with short payment histories. This is because a longer payment history allows analysts time to discern payment patterns, which are usually more predictable and stronger.

Marketability of Mortgages

The growing secondary market has created several trends which are all responses to the continuing need to increase the marketability of mortgages.

Standardization. Secondary markets will generally have standards, if not requirements, for mortgage quality and terms. Model contracts have been prepared by the nation's two major purchasers of residential mortgagers: Federal National Mortgage Corporation and the Federal Home Loan Mortgage Corporation. The Federal Housing Administration has also standardized its contracts for government insured mortgages. These standardized documents are widely used. However, they are sometimes too generalized for lenders wishing to accommodate customer demand for more flexibility.

Loan documentation standards and standardization facilitates loan liquidity and salability. It is much easier for investors to understand and estimate the risk of loans which have standardized documentation. This standardization of contracts also lead to increasing standardization of loan terms and conditions, as well as more standard underwriting criteria. This reflects the trend that many new loans are originated with marketability in mind; even existing mortgages are often reconfigured to increase their salability.

Segregation of Functions. The separation of the origination, ownership, selling and servicing aspects of mortgage lending enables greater access to the secondary mortgage market. It allows institutions to specialize in one or several areas of expertise. It also attracts institutions which want to participate in the business but which do not wish to perform some of the functions associated with mortgage banking.

Pooling. Pooling consolidates many individual mortgages of small amounts. It also makes mortgages marketable to sophisticated investors looking for large transactions. Some mortgage lenders already have investors lined up for mortgage loans before they originate them. Therefore, they tailor the loans to meet the investors' needs. Smaller volume generators can sell their loans to mortgage wholesalers and thereby gain access to a larger pool of loans. This, in turn, provides them with access to the capital markets.

Pooling may be used to create investment vehicles which diversify credit risk across regions and loan sizes. It can reduce or isolate risk in one geographic region, depending on the degree of geographic distribution of the loans. The size and diversity of the mortgage pools, which often range from $30 million to $50 million, facilitates managing the degree of credit risk.

The risk level of a mortgage pool is often structured to meet market demands. There is a wide array of risk segregating mortgage pool products. For instance, prepayment risk is reduced through the used of Collateralized Mortgage Obligations (CMOs) and Stripped Mortgage-Backed Securities. Maturity risk can be isolated through a selection of long-term and/or short-term loans. Shorter-term securities enhance quality and reduce risk by enabling the purchaser to avoid the loan's long-term exposure to default and the potential for refinancing difficulties at maturity. Shorter-term loans are easier to sell and are often structured according to standardized documentation. In contrast, longer term loans are generally more difficult to standardize due to the greater demand for unique loan terms at longer maturities.

Servicing Can Be a Low-Cost/High-Profit Operation

Servicing can be divided into seven key functional areas: customer service, remittance processing, escrow analysis/tax and insurance bills, investor reporting, collections, foreclosure, and payoff. Servicing areas which contain the highest concentration of employees are the areas where it is easiest to lower costs: customer service (12 percent), escrow analysis/ tax and insurance bills (16 percent), collections (10 percent), and foreclosure (8 percent).[7]

The key to high productivity, and therefore lower costs, in customer service is minimizing the "down time" of each representative. There is, however, a trade-off between optimal efficiency and a high level of customer service. In some cases a slightly higher average waiting time, even a few seconds more, can produce measurable gains in productivity with minimal perceived loss of customer service quality. Customer needs will determine the appropriate balance between customer waiting time and optimal utilization of personnel. The productivity gains from longer waiting times, higher abandon rates and turnaround times should be balanced against customer perceptions of service quality.

Automation is another avenue which can produce gains in productivity. Advanced systems can improve efficiency by facilitating quick and easy access to customer information. Automated voice response (AVR) enables fewer employees to answer a greater number of calls. The capital expenditure to install an AVR

---

7 Waino H. Pihl and Michael L. Wambay, "Mortgage Servicing: Rise Above the Productivity Plateau," *Bank Management,* July, 1991, pp. 26–33.

system is worthwhile since the more efficient users have systems which handle more than 60 percent of incoming calls solely through AVR.

Efficiency in escrow operations is built on effective payment of tax and insurance bills. Escrow productivity can be enhanced through segregation of duties. Tasks can be divided into receipt, entry, tracking and payment of bills, and monitoring of impound account balances. Tax bill payments are currently the most efficient area because of the ability to use tax service providers and tape-to-tape payment. A mortgage servicing operation can focus on automated tape-to-tape payments and achieve a lower cost structure without the use of a tax servicer. This route demands extensive training of personnel as well as a continued emphasis on productivity. Automated bill payment can eliminate or greatly reduce the need for manual payment of bills, reducing labor costs and improving efficiency. Automated bill payment can also improve interest earnings since servicers are able to hold escrow balances longer, taking advantage of the interest paid during the float time, before making payments.

Collections departments which achieve high productivity focus on automation and standardization. One common inefficiency is that collectors begin calling delinquent borrowers a specific number of days after payment is due but do not analyze a borrower's payment history before calling. Collectors are often assigned a number of accounts which they dial manually. Collections operations can be standardized with automated systems which track and prioritize calls. These systems can also automatically make phone calls to delinquent accounts in order of priority. This enables collections personnel to focus on accounts where a collection call is truly necessary and maximize the time collectors spend talking with delinquent borrowers.

Automation also enhances the productivity of foreclosure departments. Foreclosure tracking systems monitor all aspects of the process: monitoring workflow, assuring completion of critical tasks, helping prevent missing critical filing deadlines, and monitoring processor performance. It has been found that productivity of foreclosure processors does not depend on the type of loans serviced or portfolio makeup.[8] Many high-productivity servicers handle a variety of loan types and geographic mixes. They attribute their efficiency to using a processor, rather than an assembly line system, in conjunction with a highly automated foreclosure tracking system.

Foreclosure productivity is enhanced when one processor is responsible for the entire foreclosure process, from referral to real estate owned. This start-to-finish process has been found to be more productive because it eliminates bottlenecks at

---

8   Pihl and Wambay, "Mortgage Servicing."

various stages, encourages accountability, and generally makes the process easier to manage. This more efficient method of foreclosure may well be worth the investment of time and training required, especially for lower productivity servicers.

Enhancing Profits through Servicing: Revenues through Float, Fees and Cross-Selling

Mortgage servicers can benefit from revenues generated by maximizing float earnings on monthly payments and escrow account balances, collection of late fees, and cross-selling opportunities.

Float. Automation is one of the primary techniques used to maximize float earnings. Automated processing of funds through lockbox, automated clearinghouse (ACH), and other means speeds a higher volume of payments through the system. This enables an institution to receive funds availability as quickly as possible. Manual payments cost three to five times as much to process as automated payments, in addition to the cost of unavailable funds.[9]

Escrow balances also provide float earnings. The most critical aspect of escrow is the accuracy and quality of analysis which ensures that accounts are neither under- nor over-escrowed. A general guideline for high-quality servicers is to anticipate average escrow balances of approximately 1 percent of unpaid principal balances.[10] Two factors which influence escrow balance levels are the percentage of the portfolio escrowed and the frequency of tax payments. Escrowing a slightly higher percentage of the portfolio and paying taxes only once a year can yield substantial returns. Thrifts should keep in mind, though, that accurate escrow analysis is critical to avoiding impound advances on non-delinquent loans and maintaining customer satisfaction.

Generation of escrow income is often accomplished through net funding of loans. The servicer pays insurance, taxes, and closing costs for the borrower out of loan proceeds. In the process, the servicer earns interest on the float. Net funding of loans also lowers credit risk by ensuring that borrowers remain current on their required payments. It is also a service customers are willing to pay for in the loan's pricing. Implementing a process for the net funding of loans requires an educated staff and strong computer systems to track and write checks.

---

9 Pihl and Wambay, "Mortgage Servicing."

10 Pihl and Wambay, "Mortgage Servicing."

Late Fee Collections. Servicers that are able to minimize the time required to collect late fees benefit from enhanced current income. They also avoid having to finance the late fees as a receivable. Billing for late fees is controversial, but it can be effective. The cost of billing must be balanced with the benefit of the expected collections.

Cross-Selling. Thrifts which service mortgages have many opportunities to cross-sell because of their access to information on borrowers. This credit information can be used to pre-qualify or identify prospective borrowers, for example, for consumer or installment loans. Origination costs and credit risk are reduced substantially in these situations because of the synergisms in gathering and evaluating credit information. While many lenders are aware of the benefits of cross-selling, few put the practice into action. Cross-selling efforts for servicers can make use of the information and personnel already in place. Examples of cross-selling programs which have been effective are direct mail campaigns, 800 number loan-by-phone centers, and formal cross-selling programs with incentives for customer service agents.

Refinancers are another potential source of cross sales. Especially when interest rates are low and many borrowers refinance their homes, thrifts can easily attempt to retain servicing rights. Servicers are in a good position to identify potential refinancers within their own portfolio since they have access to loan interest-rate information. This makes it easy to target borrowers with relatively high interest rates.

Payoff is another time when the servicer can attempt to refinance either the current or a future home. Personnel who handle payoff requests can be trained or use scripting to ensure that they attempt to capture refinancers.

Cross-selling a refinancing is also cost effective. The servicer eliminates the origination fee, saving up to 50 basis points. Application processing costs are lower, too, since much of the required information is already in the servicer's database.

Risks in Entering the Secondary Mortgage Market

Pipeline/Interest Rate Risk

Pipeline risk is a major threat to a mortgage banking operation's profitability. Effective hedging of pipeline risk is often the key to profitability. Hedging can prevent losses in the short term and lower a bank's cost of capital in the long term by reducing risk.

Pipeline risk, or interest rate risk, begins when the borrower's interest rate is set (the "rate lock"). The nature and degree of that risk depends on the timing of the rate lock. Rates can be set either at closing or prior to closing.

Most grantors of mortgages set rates prior to closing. They are, in effect, purchasing mortgages on an optional delivery basis from home buyers. When a company sets a mortgage rate prior to closing, it has granted a put. In other words, it has given the home buyer the right (but not the obligation) to put (sell) the mortgage to the financial institution.

The interest rate risk attached to setting rates prior to closing is high in volatile rate environments. For example, if rates decline, a borrower is likely to decide not to close; and if rates increase or remain the same, the probability that the borrower will close is high. The value of a mortgage improves if rates decrease and declines if rates increase. Banks which do not hedge their mortgages and do not charge fees for taking on the pipeline risk of a rate lock prior to closing are placing themselves in a high-risk position.

Specific hedging vehicles include forward and future sales. These also introduce other risks, depending on the hedging instrument chosen. Investor risk, product risk, and basis risk occur in the act of hedging. Forward sales, when a mortgage originator enters a contract to deliver an established amount of a specific type of mortgage or mortgage-backed security at an agreed upon price and date, protect sellers from interest rate risk, product risk, and basis risk. Forward sales can be accomplished through whole loan sales or through mortgage-backed securities.

Whole loans sales are commonly executed through Fannie Mae and Freddie Mac, the primary outlets for conventional conforming mortgages. Private conduits are becoming an increasingly popular outlet for non-conforming mortgages. Additionally, thrifts and other institutional investors purchase significant quantities of conforming, non-conforming, and government FHA/VA mortgages.

Mortgage-backed securities (MBS) are provided by several outlets. Fannie Mae MBS and Freddie Mac PCs are the primary security vehicles for conforming mortgages. Ginnie Maes are the principal security vehicle for FHA/VA mortgages. AA rated securities are a primary outlet for non-conforming mortgages.

In addition to originating mortgages and selling the same type in the secondary market, mortgage originators can perform a substitute sale. Originators can sell alternative assets as a temporary substitute for the sale of a hedged asset. Substitute sales may be preferable to direct sales in several situations. It may not be possible or practical to sell the original mortgage in the marketplace. It may be more profitable to achieve a higher price through a substitute sale. Standardized hedge vehicles, such as futures, are often more liquid instruments than the hedged asset, giving the hedging institution more flexibility to respond to changing market conditions.

There are several other ways to minimize pipeline risk. One obvious alternative is making the time between rate setting and closing as short as possible. A speedy approval process can contribute to shortening that time frame. The longer it takes to approve and process a loan, the longer the bank is exposed to risk. Another element is the timing of the rate lock. Rather than locking in rates at the time of application, mortgage bankers can set rates, for instance, only after the application has been processed and the borrower has been qualified or within a set time period prior to closing.

Setting rates at closing eliminates the interest rate risk, but it may not be desirable in some markets. The uncertainty regarding the exact interest rate could dissuade potential borrowers from closing mortgages. Also, market competition may dictate that rates must be determined earlier. An alternative to postponing the rate lock until closing is to use a rate cap. A cap protects the borrower from increasing rates and allows the mortgage banker to plan a rate for match funding earlier.

Pipeline behavior should be analyzed before selecting risk reduction strategy. Variables that influence pipeline behavior include interest rate changes, time until closing, type of loan, competition, and demographics. Changes in interest rates relative to the rate lock affect the probability of closing. If market rates increase relative to the rate lock, the probability of closing goes up; if rates decrease, the probability of closing goes down. As the time until closing decreases, the probability of closing increases. Refinancing loans are more sensitive to interest rate changes than loans used for initial purchase. Adjustable-rate mortgages (ARMs) may be more or less likely to close than fixed-rate loans, depending on their rate levels. Competition offering aggressive, below market rates to attract business can also increase fallout. Some geographic markets are much more sensitive to small changes in interest rates than others; therefore, fallout patterns are not geographically uniform.

Origination Costs: Brick and Mortar Overhead

As discussed above, mortgage origination is costly. A large mortgage banking staff is needed to generate a high volume of originations. In addition to personnel overhead, the staff must have office space which is another substantial fixed expense.

One way to defray most costs is to become a correspondent originator and generate mortgages for larger institutions (some say a minimum of $25 million in mortgages per month must be generated in order to achieve acceptable profitability hurdles.) A thrift can also increase its mortgage origination capabilities without increasing overhead by using mortgage brokers. Depending upon the degree of independence of the mortgage brokers, they can provide varying degrees of service to the thrift. The more service they provide, the more overhead the thrift saves, yet the smaller the profits associated with the transaction. On the low-service end, mortgage brokers can originate mortgages on the thrift's forms to be processed by the thrift. On the high service end of the spectrum, a mortgage broker closes loans originated on his or her own forms, with his or her own lines of credit and delivers the documentation to the thrift, which immediately purchases the loan.

Credit Quality

A thrift must have uncompromising, clear and reasonable underwriting standards. These need to be well communicated to originators including brokers and bankers, if appropriate, and incorporate secondary marketing department requirements to the extent practical. Much like the origination function in a traditional thrift, knowledge of the local community greatly enhances credit quality, as do the quality and guidelines of the appraisal staff.

Prepayment

Prepayment risk is a source of uncertainty. The majority of residential mortgage loans allow the borrower to prepay the loan balance at any time during the term of the loan, at the borrower's discretion. Borrowers typically prepay loans to obtain refinancing when interest rates fall. From the mortgage holder's point of view, that is the worst time to recover the loan principal because the proceeds must be reinvested at a lower rate of return than when the loan was originated.

The likelihood of loan prepayment or default of fixed-rate, single family loans can be estimated, and the secondary markets discount the price of the security by an amount appropriate to compensate. Since lenders have had many years of experience with these types of loans, investors have a basis for evaluating prepayment risk. Guarantees and insurance for prepayment and default are available in the marketplace. Default insurance is available on individual loans from FHA and private insurers. Timely payment for entire mortgage pools is guaranteed by the Government National Mortgage Association or by the issuer.

8

Asset Securitization: Changing the Fundamentals of the Lending Business

Introduction

Asset securitization changed the fundamentals of consumer and mortgage lending. Its impact cannot be ignored when entry into any type of consumer lending is contemplated.

What bank chief executive has not looked over the balance sheet and dreamed of ways to turn low-balance, long-term, illiquid assets into high profit, liquid ones? Who has not contemplated addressing gap problems by simply getting those assets off the books? Many banks turn this dream into reality through the securitization of assets. Almost any loan can be securitized, including car loans, credit card receivables, and commercial loans. To date, the most frequently securitized loans have been residential mortgages which are the largest pool of assets, with longer maturities for most financial institutions.

The growing popularity of securitizing mortgages has been fueled by a real and pressing need. In 1965, when one-year T-bills were at 4.06 percent it seemed like good business sense to issue 30-year fixed-rate mortgages at an average yield of 5.74 percent. That yielded a favorable spread of 168 basis points. Based on what they knew then, many thrifts and commercial banks loaded up with these 30-year fixed-rate mortgages; then the short-term cost of funds went through the roof. Certain thrifts had all of their assets locked into these low-yielding, long-term instruments that were funded by short-term liabilities, resulting in a drastic maturity mismatch. Securitization helped many such institutions liquidate these long-term assets and redeploy the funds in a way that reduced their interest rate gap and improved their yield performance.

Asset-backed securities are a major advance from the private transactions which commercial banks and finance companies are used to. They are different from traditional loan participations, loan syndications, or discounted loan sales in that they represent the creation of marketable fixed-rate investment grade obligations. The securities, as a result, are very liquid and trade at spreads of 50 to 100 basis points over comparable Treasury obligations.

Assets securitization has become an important financing technique for banks to improve their balance sheets as well as to meet their regulatory capital requirements. Capital compliance is even more critical since the introduction of risk-based capital. Asset securitization provides the banking industry with another tool to manage its interest rate risk and restructure its balance sheets while freeing substantial amounts of capital to support growth and to reach compliance with capital requirements.

Asset securitization involves selling a portion of the loan portfolio to investors.

A new generation of asset-backed securities has been created to facilitate this strategy. These securities are conceptually similar to mortgage-backed securities but they are backed instead by financial assets other than mortgages. These may be automobile or credit card receivables that have a predetermined payment stream and an average life of more than one year. Asset securitization refers to the process of raising funds through the issuance of marketable securities backed by future cash flow from income producing assets. The economic effect of asset securitization may be described as the conversion of income producing assets into marketable securities.

These securities typically represent undivided certificates of ownership in a pool of assets being sold, including the security interest in the underlying collateral. The assets eligible for pooling have expanded beyond mortgages to include automobiles. (Both loans, are being considered for the next wave of asset securitization.) The resulting securities differ from other types of securities in that their creditworthiness depends, primarily, on the issuance of a stream of cash flow other than on the credit strength of the issuer or the market value of the collateral.

Since the first public asset-backed security offering in March of 1985 (Sperry computer leases) there have been only 120 public offerings of more than $36 billion from 1985 through 1989. This market is still in its infancy but has been estimated by Standard & Poor's to grow to $100 billion by the year 1993. Whereas asset-backed financing was once looked upon as an avenue of last resort for cash-strapped companies, it is recognized today as a powerful corporate finance and bank funding tool. Through securitization, banks can originate and service assets that are removed from their balance sheets. This new asset/liability management tool frees up capital, reduces interest rate risk and, in many situations, increases shareholder value.

Issuance of mortgage-backed and other asset-backed securities by banks has been growing rapidly both in dollar volume and in asset type diversity. Those banks with mortgage banking affiliates have securitized conforming mortgage-backed securities, plus $7.5 billion in asset-backed securities (primarily car loans and credit cards) were issued by commercial banks (Table 8–1). Commercial real estate mortgages, home equity lines of credit, lease receivables, insurance products, and possibly commercial loans offer product expansion opportunities beyond auto and credit card receivables and non-conforming residential mortgages.

The benefits of securitization are many. It offers banks a means to achieve regulatory compliance, improve asset/liability management, and to increase return on shareholder equity. For banks to achieve these strategic gains, however, they must first overcome management hurdles and build the skills necessary to adapt their business systems.

The rationale for securitization may be better understood in the context of the functions banks perform in order to add value. Banks originate, service, and fund. They may possess a competitive advantage in any one of these three functions. Traditionally, these functions were bundles, and asset size and growth were the main vehicle to achieve greater competitive advantage. These profitability dynamics have changed drastically since the factor market and regulatory deregulation. Size is no longer the only vehicle to achieve superior profits; due to capital constraints and other reasons, off-balance-sheet strategies become more important than ever.

Table 8–1: The U.S. Public Market of Receivable-Backed Securities

Summary

◆ 63 public issues since 3/85
   42 pass-throughs
   19 pay-throughs
   2 preferred stocks

◆ 9 types of collateral
   43 with autos and/or light trucks
   7 with credit cards
   5 with leases
   2 with trade receivables
   1 with airplanes
   1 corporate junk bond
   1 unsecured consumer loan
   1 mortgage-backed and corporate security

◆ $22.3 billion total

Source: *Journal of Equipment Lease Financing,* 1988

The Securitization Process

Background

The securitization process can transform an illiquid loan into a marketable security. It is essentially an extension of the mortgage finance market. Since 1970 the mortgage finance market has been securitizing real estate assets via pass-through securities representing ownership of individual shares in a pool of mortgages. This technique gave mortgage bankers the cash to write still more mortgages and it created a new security that a typical investor could buy and sell. As much as 80 percent of new single family home mortgages are now being securitized and sold into the secondary market. The success of this market has clearly influenced the introduction of new forms of securitized assets.

Qualifications for Securitization

Certain structural characteristics of the underlying assets selected make securitization easier. The majority of securitized assets include mostly consumer-related loans, largely because of the standardization and consistency which exist within the consumer loan business.

The basic goal of securitization is to create a pool that can be structured in such a way as to obtain a rating from the rating agencies, thereby making the securities marketable. The following are several asset characteristics that facilitate securitization:

1. Standardized loan documentation

2. Extensive payment delinquency and loss history computed on a consistent basis

3. Fixed interest rate or yield

4. Fully amortized payment stream

5. Geographic diversity

6. Seasoning (age of assets)

7. Standardized, high-quality credit underwriting and collection policies

8. High-quality collateral

There are also characteristics that detract from the attractiveness of assets as securitization candidates. These are:

1. Inexperienced or under capitalized servicer

2. Small number of assets in pool

3. High ratio of largest asset to average asset

4. Balloon maturities

5. Ability of obligors to change payment dates

6. Infrequent payment dates[1]

---

1   Everette D. Hull, *The Complete Story On Securitization of Bank Assets Part I*, Robert Morris Associates, p. 23

As mentioned, many types of assets have been securitized. Among them are the following:

♦ Equipment

♦ Auto loans

♦ Credit cards

♦ Truck loans

♦ Commercial real estate loans

♦ Manufactured housing loans

♦ Installment sales contracts

♦ Government supported loan programs, Small Business Administration loans, and FHA farm loans

♦ Home equity loans

♦ Boat loans

♦ Non-performing loans

♦ Recreational vehicles

♦ Municipal equipment leasing

♦ Tax exempt industrial development bonds

The proliferation of asset types and issuers of asset-backed securities is growing exponentially. However banks, thrifts, and finance companies still dominate the issuance market (see Table 8-2).

The Process

Securitization is a carefully structured process whereby loans and other receivables are packaged, underwritten, and sold in the form of securities. The process can be broken into the following components:

1. *Origination.* Securitization begins when a company originates and puts together a pool of underlying primary assets. Those assets can be sold either as

Table 8–2: Typical Asset-Based Securitization Issues

Product/Characteristics	Residential Mortgages	Auto Loans	Credit Cards	Commerical Real Estate Mortgages	C&I Loans
Site	$150–500 K	$5–50 K	$1–10 K	$50 K–$50 MM	$100 K–50 MM
Collateral	1–4 family homes	Automobiles	—	Commercial properties	Plant, equipment, company stock, personal guarantees, etc.
Features	–Easily valued –Marketable	–Easily valued –Marketable	Easily valued –Somewhat marketable	–Easily valued –Marketable	–Difficult to value –Not always marketable
Gross Spread	1–2%	1–2%	6–12%	1–2%	0–2%
Interest rate basis	Fixed, adjustable	Fixed	Fixed, adjustable	Fixed	Adjustable
Typical credit enhancement	Senior/sub	3rd party guarantee	3rd party guarantee	Senior/sub	3rd party guarantee
REMIC Election	Yes	No	No	Yes	No

specific receivables, in which case they have a fixed maturity, or can be created from accounts whose balances revolve over time, such as credit card receivables.

2. *Structuring.* Typically, the originator then sells the pool of assets to a special purpose vehicle set up for the purpose of structuring the transaction. The special purpose vehicle (which can be a trust, special limited partnership or a special purpose corporation) determines the tax and accounting structure of the transaction and structures the relevant operational details such as the payment characteristics of the note and protection against bankruptcy risk. There are several basic structures which have been used by companies to securitize assets. The choice of structure depends on the characteristics of the receivables and the objectives of the issuer as well as economic, accounting, legal, tax, and marketing considerations. The two vehicles most commonly used are illustrated in Figure 8–1.

Pass-Through Structure

The pass through structure is the most commonly used format of asset sales. In this structure the owner of the assets sells the receivables to a trust. That trust is formed for the sole purpose of purchasing the assets and issuing the securities. The securities are pass-through certificates which represent a fractional undivided interest in a pool of receivables held by the trust. The grantor trust is a passive structure in terms of tax treatment and restructuring the cash flows from the receivables, as well as in managing the assets sold to the trust. The advantage of the pass-through structure is that there are no capitalization requirements for the issuer.

Pay-Through Structure

A pay-through structure is used when the seller forms the special purpose vehicle (SPV) mentioned above. The SPV is either owned by the seller or, in some cases, an unrelated party. The seller will sell or pledge the receivables to the SPV which, in turn, issues a debt instrument collateralized by the receivables. The SPV is structured as a limited purpose vehicle thus insulating the investors from the bankruptcy and financial risks of both the seller and the SPV. It allows for flexible structuring of the cash flow from the receivables. This flexibility can be used for various purposes, including taking advantage of the yield curve through a modified collateralized mortgage obligation. For tax purposes the asset-backed security must be treated as debt.

Figure 8–1: Cash Flows
Pass-Through and Pay-Through Securitization Process

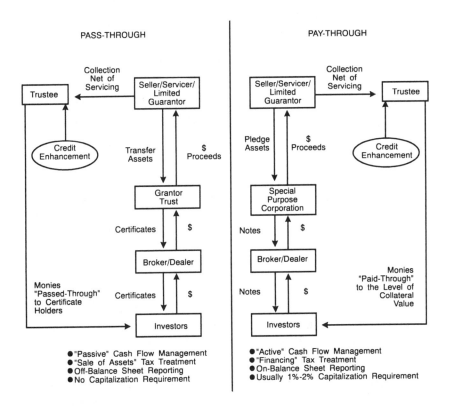

PASS-THROUGH

- "Passive" Cash Flow Management
- "Sale of Assets" Tax Treatment
- Off-Balance Sheet Reporting
- No Capitalization Requirement

PAY-THROUGH

- "Active" Cash Flow Management
- "Financing" Tax Treatment
- On-Balance Sheet Reporting
- Usually 1%-2% Capitalization Requirement

Source: *Journal of Equipment Lease Financing,* Vol. 6 No. 1, 1988.

3. *Credit Enhancement.* Some form of credit investment procedure is typically necessary to obtain an investment credit rating and make the transaction attractive to investors. The SPV generally obtains insurance to guarantee a portion of the potential losses of the assets. This guarantee is typically in the form of a first loss guarantee (often in the form of a spread account) from the originator of the primary assets, in conjunction with a wrap guarantee (similar to an reinsurance in the property casualty business). The reason credit enhancement is required is that the securities almost always are required to achieve AA or AAA rating. Without such rating, the transaction may be difficult to complete. There are several methods to obtain the requisite credit support:

◆ Over-collateralization, including a senior/junior structure, in which a certain percentage of the debt issued is subordinated.

◆ Recourse obligations to the issuer (provided the issuer is rated AA or AAA).

◆ Insurance, letter of credit, or surety bonds from an AA or AAA entity.

◆ A combination of the above, such as collateralizing a letter of credit with a spread account in which a percentage of cash flows from the transaction is escrowed until the cash collateral reaches a specific level. The proceeds of the spread account revert to the seller when the bonds have amortized completely. A spread account can also be used to strengthen an issuer's guarantee or over-collateralization.

4. *Placement and Trading.* The SPV or a third party, usually the underwriter, then issues notes that are very highly rated. These notes are usually bought by institutional investors. Mutual funds are the single most important group of such investors in the asset-based securities market today. Pricing considerations play an important role in placement and trading. The factors affecting the price of each transaction are complex and specific to each issue. Generally, five major components enter into pricing considerations.

◆ Spread over Treasuries. Asset-backed securities are priced at a fixed spread over the yield of the Treasury security which best approximates the average life of the underlying receivables. This is the single most volatile piece in the pricing equation. Yield levels may rise or fall sharply between the time at which a company begins to consider the asset-based security financing and the date when the issue is actually priced. The Treasury rate can be fixed or capped using a variety of techniques, most of which involve the hedging instruments described in the first part of this book. This is a perfect example where a forward swap, a forward rate, a zero cost option, and other hedging vehicles could freeze the cost of funds for an asset-based transaction.

Securitized debt does not necessarily trade at the same spread over Treasuries as comparably rated straight debt. The primary factor impacting this spread is the investor's comfort with the cash flow certainty. If investors doubt the predictability of the cash flow because of the likelihood of prepayments, then the spread over Treasuries for the issue will be higher than the spread for corporate debt of a similar rating. Since assets with longer average life and weighted average maturity will be expected to have more risk of prepayment, they may be more costly. Conversely, investors may be uneasy with an issue whose average life is considerably shorter than the longest final maturity of an asset in the pool, which shows a consistent and manageable percentage of historical delinquencies and defaults.

Leases present different considerations for investors. Whereas a typical auto loan transaction involves loans to individual obligators with actuarial diversity, the auto lease transaction typically involves corporate lessors and lessees. More attention is focused on the corporate credits, especially in view of the residual value assumptions built into the lease. These assumptions carry a risk borne on the back end of the transaction by the lessor or the investor. In a loan, the downpayment forces the obligor to assume comparable risk on the front end.

◆ Credit enhancement. As mentioned above, the majority of securitization transactions still need credit enhancements to achieve the desired credit ratings to satisfy investors. The amount of enhancement will vary depending on the credit of the obligor and the quality of the collateral. For example, private partnership notes representing only the good faith obligation of the partner would require more enhancement for the debt issue than a portfolio of car loans with credit histories and underlying collateral, or an issue originated by a household name company. The cost of credit enhancement is also impacted by the type used. A parent company guarantee is less expensive than a third party guarantee of a debt issue, although the latter may be better perceived by investors.

◆ Public versus private debt. In addition to a well documented, predictable payment history and a good delinquency and default record, the issuer can improve pricing of a securitized debt issue by making it a public versus a private issue. Publicly issued securities are more liquid than privately issued securities and, consequently, carry a lower coupon in most markets. However, public issues are much more costly to issue and administer and less flexible in timing of the offering.

◆ Legal, accounting, trustee and underwriting fees. The amount of professional fees paid for services needed to complete the debt issue impacts pricing as well. These fees will be higher or lower depending upon the complexity of the structure of the transaction and whether it is public or private.

Prior to issuing a rating for the asset-backed securities, the rating agencies determine their rating based upon the following concerns:

◆ Credit quality

◆ Expected default rate

◆ Equity component and/or credit enhancement

◆ Liquidity

◆ Maturity gap between assets and liabilities

◆ Structure

◆ Bankruptcy remote issuer

◆ True sale of receivables to issuer

◆ Servicer risk

◆ Independent servicer

◆ Segregated cash flows

5. *Servicing.* The underlying assets can be serviced either by a third party or by the originator who retains the spread between the yield on the assets and the interest paid to the investor's net of credit enhancement and other fees. Many banks use asset securitization to generate such servicing fees and create servicing portfolios off their balance sheets, thereby significantly enhancing their fee income.

The Benefits of Securitization

Securitization is an effective tool to address many management and risk-related issues It is particularly relevant in the context of managing overall bank profitability and balance sheet restructuring. Securitization is a tool than can address profitability issues, capital requirements issues and asset/liability management problems:

1. *Asset Quality Issues.* The banking industry has experienced significant asset quality problems over the last few years. The resulting squeeze on bank profitability has taken its toll on the value of bank stocks and the perception of safety by customers, regulators in the investment community, and overall market valuation. Securitization permits banks to unload, albeit at a cost, low-quality assets, thereby cleaning their balance sheets and redeploying their resources in more profitable assets.

2. *Improved Capital Position.* Capital requirements of banks have become more and more stringent in recent years, culminating in the risk-based capital requirements put in place in January 1, 1992. Securitization can be used to address capital requirements issues. If a securitization transaction is structured and accounted for as a sale of the underlying assets, the transaction results in a reduction of both assets and liabilities and the net effect is to increase the banks's overall capital ratio. In addition, some transactions allow the bank to sell its assets at a premium which results in booking net income. In such cases there is a "double injection" of capital to improve the bank's capitalization. This may be an essential component in many banks' strategies toward meeting their regulatory capital adequacy requirements. Last, a sale of assets releases capital for the generation of new assets thereby, providing relief with respect to asset growth and generation of quality earning assets.

3. *Securitization as a Funding Source.* Securitization, in effect, creates a new source of funds for the issuing bank. Securitization is an internal source of funding under the control of the issuing bank, and can replace deposit gathering as a way to obtain low-cost funds. As traditional low-cost funding sources such as demand deposits and savings are stagnant or showing decelerated growth, and as competition for deposits intensifies by mutual funds and other financial and non-depository institutions, the addition of a funding source through asset securitization could

significantly enhance the financial flexibility of the bank without impairing its access to traditional funding sources. The cost of securitization as a funding source can also be favorable. Through the credit enhancement vehicle, an A or a BBB rated bank can issue a AA or AAA security at AAA interest rates. These can be as low as 60 to 80 basis points higher than comparable maturities of U.S. Treasury Notes, as Bank of America (rated BBB at the time) found out in 1987. This low-cost alternative can be much more cost effective than other debt and preferred stock alternatives available to the bank.

Also, unlike debt or equity financing, asset securitization, in effect, raises funds without incurring the costs of raising additional equity capital. These costs including dividends to shareholders, taxes, reserve requirements, and deposit insurance are eliminated with securitized transactions. These heavy costs by far outweigh the costs of securitization. The cost of intermediating an asset-backed security including structuring fees, marketing costs, credit enhancement, and other costs of issuance are typically about 25 basis points per year over the life of the security. If a commercial bank were to hold the same size loan portfolio, the holding costs associated with the portfolio including taxes, deposit insurance, dividends, and reserve requirements would be about 150 basis points.

4. *Profitability Enhancement.* For many years a traditional source of bank profitability has been lending money. However, as net interest margins experience additional pressures, the profitability of the lending business, which involves origination funding and holding to maturity, has been declining since the late 1970s. Although net interest margins have remained relatively unchanged, loan risk has been increasing dramatically and with it, default rates. This is, in part, the result of intensified competition for the banks' most creditworthy customers and the disintermediation of some of these customers which are now using the commercial paper markets as a short-term funding source. The resulting pressures on bank profitability have been reflected in depressed stock prices.

A study on bank profitability by the Federal Reserve Bank of New York found that bank profits declined during 1980 to 1985 because of economic factors such as higher inflation, interest rate volatility, and growing loss provisions, but also structural changes such as the decline of wholesale lending, deposit interest rate deregulation, and a secular up-trend in loan loss provisions to reflect the increasing risk of banks' lending portfolios.

The impact of the commercial paper market on the decline of wholesale lending was also significant. Most corporations had access to that market and could fund themselves either by issuing of commercial paper or low-grade bonds. The remaining companies were either illiquid, small, or risky. Even many of those could use credit enhancement to gain access to the public debt markets at rates that reflected the guarantors' credit rating, thereby disintermediating the banks.

Banks have been forced to look for new ways to combat these problems while being restricted by banking laws and regulations and accounting rules in a way that inhibits their ability to effectively compete in the capital markets. Loan sale in the form of securitization is a profitability enhancement tool. On the one hand, the selling bank continues to collect an interest rate differential resulting from the loan rate less the pass-through rate on the securities and less any ongoing expenses. Since the assets are removed from the balance sheet, this creation of fee income results in an improved return on assets and return on equity for the issuing bank.

5. *Asset/Liability Management.* Asset securitization can be an effective tool for asset/liability management. The sale of securities is an outright simple instrument which can alter the maturity mix of the asset side of the balance sheet. Further, the funding sources created by asset securitization enable the issuer to clearly identify the funding cost associated with a specific asset by matching the sale proceeds with the security itself or the new assets purchased (the issuer can elect to hold the security or convert it to cash and buy other assets with the proceeds).

The average life of the asset matches the average life of the securitized liabilities which are used to finance these assets. Securitization, therefore, can be used to match fund assets with equal maturity liabilities. For example, the proceeds from the securitization and sale of auto loans can be used to fund new auto loans at more competitive interest rates to customers because the bank is not planning to hold the assets, namely the car loans with the funding costs associated with financing those particular assets.

Securitization, particularly involving a loan sale which is funded soon after origination, also provides a hedge against interest rate risk by eliminating the spread income and replacing it with fee income. This is particularly attractive in times of volatile interest rates and uncertain capital markets direction. Since the issuing bank has the option to continue to service the securitized assets, significant fee income can also be generated.

6. *Risk-Based Capital Reduction.* Loans typically carry with them high-risk based capital requirements which could range from 50 percent to 200 percent. By securitizing and selling those loans off the balance sheet, the risk-based capital assessment of that particular loan pool will be eliminated and could be replaced by Treasury or agency securities which bear 0 percent to 20 percent risk-based capital. This will result in a significantly lower overall risk-based capital profile of the institution.

Securitization enables banks to eliminate regulatory costs of deposit insurance premiums, reserve requirements and capital requirements on those assets that will be removed from the balance sheet.

7. *Strategic Uses.* As banks identify strategic focus and market concentrations, asset securitization can be used to redeploy the assets not only for internal balance sheet management purposes. For example, if a bank is interested in building market share for a particular type of loan but the loan origination capacity exceeds the bank's funding growth or capitalization capabilities, asset securitization allows the bank to continue to build loan volume faster than deposit growth or capital structure will allow. Such growth can enhance market share and, therefore, profitability as well as allow the institution to leverage resident lending expertise in a specific product line. Asset sales, therefore, will permit the bank to grow a specific type of loan portfolio and be responsive to its customers' needs without the need to issue additional capital.

Another advantage associated with securitization is enhancing the bank's ability to more competitively price loan origination yields because loans that are earmarked for securitization are being funded at more competitive interest rates. This, in turn, permits volume growth and service income growth while capturing greater market share.

Benefits and Disadvantages of Asset Securitization

Benefits	Disadvantages
Acceleration of earnings	Asset growth diminished
Reduced capital requirements	Only certain assets are eligible
Increased return	Quality of balance sheet may decline
Increased effective leverage	Issue costs could be expensive
Term matched funding	Sale is a complex task
Non-interest income growth	Systems
New source of funding	– Complex Accounting and financial considerations
	– Legal
Credit enhancement fees	
Strategic uses	Accelerated earning recognition (tax implications)
Specialization	

8. *Acceleration of Earnings.* Securitization facilitates the acceleration of earnings. A portion of the net interest spread that otherwise would be realized over the life of the loan is recorded as a profit on the day of the sale. This profit represents excess servicing fees, the amount over which is necessary to service the assets through liquidation. Accounting policy permits the sold assets to be removed from the balance sheet as of the sale date, which reduces capital support requirements. The acceleration of profit and correspondent reduction in asset levels produces an improvement in return on assets and equity measures of the bank.

9. *Term Matching of Assets and Liabilities.* Another benefit of securitization is the reduction of interest rate risk. The investor in these transactions assumes the interest rate risk and the maturity profile of the assets purchased. In the sale of fixed-rate assets, the seller benefits from a fixed net interest margin between the yield from the asset and the interest rate paid to investors.

Securitization Disadvantages

Securitization is not for everyone. There are several reasons that prevent financial institutions from securitizing assets.

1. *Sale is a Complex Task.* Asset securitization can be time consuming and expensive. Substantial preparation, particularly in the computer systems and accounting areas, is required in order to securitize financial assets. All loans have to be properly documented and tapes readily available which describe the loan portfolio characteristics including weighted average coupon (WAC) and weighted average maturity (WAM).

2. *Asset Securitization as a Source of Funds.* Although the market for asset securitization is very deep and liquid, it still has a long way to go. In 1987, only 2 percent of the U.S. consumer debt has been securitized as compared to 23 percent of all the mortgages originated. Further, some banks are very efficient in deposit gathering. They can acquire deposits very efficiently and inexpensively and are likely to find the cost of securitization higher than their own origination costs. Many banks have not fully realized their potential for fund raising. While securitization may be an attractive alternative source of funds for many money center banks

and for banks in an adverse economic environment, it is less important to banks with attractive sources and uses of funds.

3. *Asset Securitization to Increase Profitability.* Many banks have very strong margins. The fee income from securitization must be sufficient to offset the continuation of favorable spreads. One-time fees may not be enough to effectively compete with a net interest margin of 500 to 550 basis points. As a result, asset securitization may need to become a way of life for an institution in order to sustain profitability. For example, mortgage banking can be profitable through continuous securitization on a superior low-cost servicing structure, but if asset securitization means that once or twice a year one removes marginal assets, the fee income does not provide an income stream sufficient to be similar to a spread. If one securitizes the plum assets, one may end up with depleted sources of core business income.

4. *Issuing Costs.* Asset securitization can be expensive. Underwriting fees for auto loan paper, for example, have typically averaged 40 basis points of the offering amount. The fees for other types of asset sales such as manufactured housing have been more than twice as high. Outside legal fees can exceed $100,000 if not properly managed. Further, some costs may be incurred in modifying computer systems to support the transaction. Fees for external auditors, the credit rating agency, registration costs and the trustee will also add to the overall cost of the transaction. In total, issuing cost to complete an initial asset securitization can reach $750,000. Because public asset securitization can be a costly process, it is recommended primarily for offerings of more than $75 million.

A more efficient alternative for smaller transactions would be a private placement or direct sale of receivables to other financial institutions or buyers. This could eliminate many of these expenses; however, the interest rate paid to investors in these alternative transactions would likely be higher than in a public securitization, to compensate for the lower liquidity of the issue. Although the cost of asset securitization appears high, this appearance diminishes when compared to the weighted cost of capital retained in the balance sheet. Table 8–3 demonstrates this without considering cost of insurance and the other elements described above.

In order to obtain the sale treatment for both generally accepted accounting principles (GAAP) and regulatory accounting principles (RAP) the loan sale must be without recourse. As a result, the financial condition of the sale is irrelevant in terms of the transactions evaluation by credit rating agencies and investors. This situation is particularly beneficial for troubled institutions that want to downsize the balance sheet through securitization. Because of the no-recourse feature of the sale, investors must rely on the cash flow from the transaction and the credit

Table 8–3: Alternative Cost Comparison

	Securitization	On-Balance Sheet Funding*
Based 2-year Treasury	8.75%	8.75%
Spread over Treasury	0.80%	—
Interest spread	—	0.65%
Total debt rate	0.50%	—
Pre-tax equity cost	—	25.00%
Weighted cost of capital	0.05%	10.18%

*5% capital ratio assumed with a 15% return on equity objective.

enhancement from another creditworthy institution to make the transaction feasible. The credit enhancement process involves a third party (a bank or an insurance company) which provides protection to investors against credit losses over and above those not covered by the cash flow from the sold assets.

Typically, the credit enhancement organization will provide credit loss protection equal to four to eight times the expected loss experience for the particular asset pool. The benefits from the credit enhancement process are many. First, without it there will be no securitization. Further, credit enhancement detaches the credit loss risk from the seller, thereby permitting regulatory accounting sale treatment. Also, the AAA or AA credit rating for the securities offered to the investors reduces the funding costs and makes that low cost available to banks which themselves are not able to support an AAA credit rating.

The cost of the credit enhancement varies. For car loan transactions, for example, the typical credit enhancement will cover 7 to 12 percent of the offering size. The letter of credit balance will decline as repayments from the transactions occur maintaining the original percentage of the reduced pool amount as the transaction liquidates. A typical letter of credit fee would equal 50 basis points of the balance. This translates into a relatively small cost of the overall transaction estimated at five basis points. Credit enhancement is not only a cost, but can become a source of income for those creditworthy banks that are prepared to offer the letter of credit to the issuing institution. Since nearly all publicly issued and debt structured asset-backed securities transactions have had sufficient credit enhancement to obtain one of the two highest ratings available, rated banks can provide letters of credit to back that sale of securities and thereby create off-balance-sheet fee income.

The institution providing the credit enhancement relies on the cash flow from the transaction and an initial deposit from the seller to act as a buffer against credit losses that may materialize after the sale. The customers make monthly payments including interest and principal to the seller or the servicer of the loans. The servicer remits all monies, except its servicing fee, to the SPV established to administer the transaction. The SPV distributes proceeds to the letter of credit bank and investors. Investors receive all principal repayments from the customer and interest at the agreed on pass-through rate. The letter of credit bank receives all other proceeds representing the net interest spread between the customer interest rate and the rate paid to the investors less the servicing rate paid to the servicers.

For example, if the customer rate were 12 percent and the transaction investor rate were 9 percent the letter of credit would receive 3 percent less the amount retained by the servicers as previously agreed (often 0.25 percent). In the event of a credit loss, the servicers notify the letter of credit bank which pays back to the trust an amount equal to the credit loss. The SPV would then forward that amount as a principal reduction in the transaction to the investors. This way the investors receive all of the principal repayments even in a credit loss situation. The letter of credit bank has used the cash flow from the transaction to pay the investor back for credit losses that took place. After the letter of credit bank satisfies its own requirements for reserves against credit losses, it can begin to pay the excess proceeds back to the seller servicers. In the car loan transactions, this generally occurs within twelve to eighteen months after the sale date.

Accelerated Earnings Realization

To determine the gain on sale that can be recorded under GAAP, a profit model is required to estimate the remaining income and cost associated with the sold assets. The model should take into consideration the estimated remaining life of the assets, including any assumptions of prepayments. Prepayment assumptions, as well as assumptions on the interest yield on the sold assets, the investor pass-through interest rate, and the servicing fee required to liquidate the loans and the credit loss provisions are all necessary in order to construct the profit model. After all these factors are determined the net excess servicing fee is present valued in accordance with GAAP in order to record the gain on sale. In this example (Table 8-4) net excess service fees booked on the sale are $4.9 million.

Table 8–4: Determination of Excess Servicing

	Profit Model (Percent)	Lifetime Amount (Mils)
Interest yield on sold assets	13.4	$22.1
Less: ABS interest rate	7.7	12.7
Servicing fee	1.6	2.7
Credit losses	0.8	1.3
Net excess service fees	3.3%	$ 5.4
Present value discount @ 7.7%		(0.5)
Excess service fees booked on sale		$ 4.9

Source: *Bank Administration,* Oct., 1988, p. 26

For regulatory accounting, the expenses associated with the sale must be deducted but there is no gain recorded at the date of the sale which results in a loss of $1.3 million, as shown in Table 8–3. The total lifetime profit ($2 million) from the transaction is the same for GAAP and RAP, but the timing difference is significant. Most of the GAAP profit is recorded as of the date of the sale, while for regulatory accounting the profits are realized over the remaining life of the deal, which may be up to five years. The major balance sheet effect on both GAAP and RAP is the removal of the sold assets from the balance sheet. Assuming a 6 percent capital ratio or a one to 15 leverage, the sale of $100 million of assets would free up $6 million worth of equity support. On the bank regulatory books, even after absorbing the $1.3 million date of sale loss the seller has net additional capital available of $4.7 million. On the GAAP books, an equity surplus of $7.4 million is achieved on the date of sale.

◆ It provides a Triple-A credit rating for securities offered to investors by firms which themselves are not able to support a Triple-A credit rating.

◆ It improves the pricing for the selling organization because the transaction is now priced as a high-grade security.

The cost of credit enhancement can vary. For auto-backed transactions, the typical credit enhancement will cover 7 percent to 10 percent of the offering size.

The letter of credit (LC) balance declines as repayments from the transaction occur, maintaining the original percentage on the reduced pool amount as the transaction liquidates.

A typical letter of credit fee would equal 0.5 percent of the L/C balance. This translates to relatively small cost in the overall transaction, estimated at about five basis points.

The credit enhancement institution relies on the cash flow from the transaction and an initial deposit from the selling organization to act as a buffer against credit losses that may materialize from the sale.

The customers make monthly payments, including interest and required principal repayment, to the seller/servicer of the loans. The servicer remits all monies except its servicing fee to the grantor trust established to administer the transaction. The trust distributes proceeds to the letter of credit bank and investors.

Investors receive all principal repayments from the customer and interest at the agreed on pass-through rate. The LC bank receives all other proceeds, representing the net interest spread between the customer interest rate and the rate paid to investors, less the servicing rate paid to the servicer. For example, if the customer rate were 13 percent and the transaction investor rate were 10 percent, the letter of credit would receive 3 percent less the amount retained by the servicer as previously agreed.

In the event a credit loss occurs, the servicer would notify the letter of credit bank, which would pay back to the trust an amount equal to the credit loss. The trust would then forward that amount as a principal reduction in the transaction to the investors. In this way, the investor receives all of his or her principal repayments, even in credit loss situations. The LC bank in essence has used cash flow from the transaction to pay the investor back for credit losses that have occurred.

After the letter of credit bank satisfies its requirements for reserves against credit losses, it will begin to pay the excess proceeds back to the seller/servicer in the form of a receivables quality servicing payment. In an auto loan transaction, this will generally occur within 12 to 18 months after the sale date.

Accounting Issues

Statement 77 of the Financial Accounting Standards Board, regarding the transfer of receivables, requires the following conditions for sale treatment under generally accepted accounting policy:

◆ The seller must surrender control of future economic benefits.

◆ The seller must be able to reasonably estimate any remaining recourse provisions for credit losses.

The requirements for regulatory accounting policy sale treatment are as follows:

◆ The transaction must be accomplished in accordance with GAAP (which means all the GAAP tests above must be met). In addition, there can be no possible negative earnings effects.

◆ There can be no future possible charge to capital, including the capital for loan loss.

◆ Any future income from the sold assets received by the seller must be non-refundable.

Bank regulatory accounting policy is more restrictive than GAAP accounting. GAAP permits sales with recourse, but RAP accounting does not; income must be reported as received in cash under RAP. This difference in accounting methods requires an ongoing accounting reconciliation until sold assets are fully liquidated.

In order to properly evaluate securitization strategies, the right incentives must be put in place for managers to make economic decisions. Key considerations may include the following:

Separating Gap Profits from Banking Business Profits. The profitability of the basic business units of the bank can be distorted by the allocation of profits or losses that arise from interest rate mismatches between that business unit's assets and liabilities. For example, if the small business loan division funds itself, at least in part, with inexpensive deposits from its small business clients, these cheap funds "subsidize" the asset portfolio, thereby creating a very wide spread. If the assets were match funded using a transfer price set by the Treasury department based upon their maturity profile, the profits may decline. Because securitization decisions involve fixed-income assets, the booked gain or loss of the sale will reflect the difference between the assets' coupon rate and the prevailing interest rates in the market at the time of securitization. The asset/liability management committee must make conscious tradeoffs between improved balance sheet management and reported earnings. For that to happen, a transfer pricing system or, at minimum, an appropriate allocation of liabilities costs to assets, must take place.

Full (including risk-based) Capital Allocation to Each Business. Decision making in banks often ignores the capital required to book assets. As a result, the actual profitability of its loan businesses is distorted. On occasion, a bank can find itself originating and holding assets that do not cover their own costs of capital because the origination and hold decisions do not consider the capital allocation implications of the assets. This is less prevailing today when risk-based capital is quickly entering the vocabulary of bank management. We have seen balance sheet restructurings that take place in order to minimize risk-based capital, particularly in the investment portfolio of the banks (when assets are shifted from higher to lower risk-based capital categories). However, full capital allocation to each asset is necessary in order to correctly understand the profitability dynamics of the asset.

Incentive Compensation. In the past banks traditionally rewarded their managers according to share volume and absolute dollar performance such as overall portfolio size or booked interest income. These measurements may not necessarily maximize the overall bank performance in terms of return on equity or on assets and have often proven to be to the detriment of overall bank performance, particularly when asset quality was not taken into account. Banks should institute incentive systems that explicitly reward actions that contribute to overall bank profitability on a capital and risk adjusted basis, such that individual performance and individual compensation are consistent with the best interests of the bank and maximize its performance.

A strong, focused Treasury function can design and implement the systems necessary to address full capital allocation and transfer pricing or proper allocation of funding costs. Incentive compensation will then follow.

Skills and Resources Required for Effective Securitization

In addition to the strategic considerations and practical elements discussed above, banks which seriously consider securitization also need to assess their in-house resources to determine where skill building is required. Among the resources necessary are the following:

◆ Capital markets competence: understanding and connections

◆ Deal structuring (technical and negotiating capability)

◆ Systems and operational support (necessary to produce the tapes, WAC and WAM items)

♦ Legal staff quality (or access to outside counsel)

♦ Private placement networks (if private issues are considered)

Those banks that do not have the in-house savvy and resources necessary in order to pull off successful securitization can use upstream correspondence in order to achieve the same objectives. These include attorneys, consultants, accountants, and other professionals, who can effectively augment gaps in in-house expertise. In addition, your correspondent bank may help.

Securitization as a Specialization Tool

As the number of securitized transactions continues to grow, technology will start to desegregate the functional roles for banks. Institutions will then be able to concentrate their efforts on one of the activities associated with the securities chain: originating, assembling, structuring, distributing or servicing. This differentiation will create greater opportunity for strategic focus among financial institutions, which will better allocate resources throughout the system altogether. They will do what they do best. Some will focus on pure origination across a very broad product line within a certain geographic area while others may opt to become national servicers or intermediaries for individual products.

As these role definitions evolve, the greater strategic focus will permit more productive competition based on distinctively different service levels or fundamentally lower costs than the head to head competition that now often characterizes the financial services industry. It could also help small institutions, such as community banks and super-community banks, survive the industry's worsening profit squeeze. Smaller banks and thrifts are often very efficient originators of credit and gatherers of savings. A credit-securitizing industry structure would permit less formidable players to focus on their high-value added customer contact roles and subcontract out the servicing, interest rate risk management, wholesale funding, and other activities in which they are ill-equipped to compete.

The securitization process (Figure 8–2) can offer strategic profit opportunities while specializing in certain functions. Once a bank originates a loan, it can retain several components of it in order to generate a profit. If it retains the loan in its own portfolio, it becomes an intermediator of credit risk and interest rate risk and for that it gets compensated. In addition to risk intermediation, the bank provides servicing facilities by billing and collecting loan payments each month. For that the bank receives fee income. Each one of these components can be retained or sold as

Figure 8–2: The Players in the Securitization Transaction

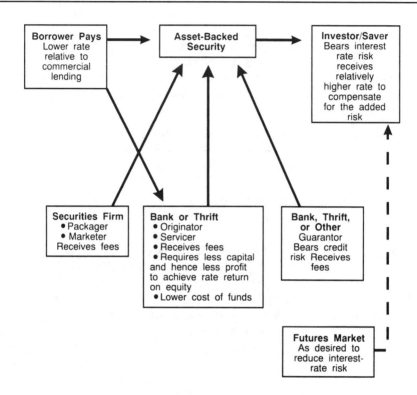

Source: *Commercial Lending Review*

part of the securitization process. If the bank sells the loan with recourse it retains the credit risk. It does not retain the interest rate risk. For that credit risk it can get compensated. If the bank sells the loans without recourse it eliminates the credit risk and the interest rate risk, however in either case the bank can opt to retain the servicing or sell it. The bank, therefore, has ultimate flexibility in decompartmentalizing the different profit elements of the lending process.

Each strategy provides a different set of potential sources of income for the lender. For example, the lender can stop short of formal securitization and still benefit through loan participations or private placements of loan portfolios. Originating a loan and then selling it without recourse responds to both the need to meet loan demand and the requirement to stay within regulated capital guidelines. Those banks that purchase all or part of the security also benefit. For them the transaction provides a way to extend credit to borrowers to whom they may not have access. It is a cost-effective way to lend money without an originating network. In addition, it is helpful to asset/liability management. By buying loans originated by another institution, payment terms can be obtained that are not otherwise available but are instrumental in managing the asset/liability gap. Securitization thereby provides greater flexibility in adjusting balance sheets and quickly responding to changes in interest rates. Figure 8–2 schematically depicts the way different players in the securitization transaction interact with one another and the role each one occupies. In addition the benefits incurred by serving in any of these roles are listed, this depiction indicates that securitization could *be* a win/win situation to all players which is the purpose of financial innovation.

Can Small Banks Participate in Securitization?

Securitization of consumer receivables, mortgages and other loans is fundamentally changing the way we do business. This is an evolutionary process that began in the 1970s and is in the process of accelerating. Banks, thrifts, and mortgage companies have been originating mortgage products for sale for years to the secondary and capital markets through third parties. As the asset-backed securities market continues to grow, the primary and secondary markets for these securities will also develop further to create greater depth in liquidity. With growing volumes, investors will become more knowledgeable about securitization and this financing technique will become more familiar. As a result, small community banks and regional banks will be able to participate. Since the lowest minimum size for a securities issue (for economic reasons) is between $75 and $100 million, a community bank by itself obviously would not have the volume of new loans to meet that constraint.

However, as the markets become more efficient, the minimum size issue will decline as we have seen in the mortgage banking business. In that business, intermediaries package loans for smaller banks into pools that are big enough to be securitized. Those intermediaries have not yet taken an active role for securitizing assets other than mortgages. The necessary infrastructure is likely to be built up by investment banks, securities firms, and also by regional banks which act as correspondents. Credit securitization can represent one of the ways that community and small banks can maintain their customer franchise and survive industry consolidation and overall transformation. Securitization offers a way out for small banks from the constraints of their balance sheets. It provides them with the opportunity to meet their customer needs on an ongoing basis with every type of credit without taking undue interest rate risk.

For example, they may include long-term fixed rate loans which otherwise may not be suitable for their loan portfolio. Small banks can now meet their customer needs almost regardless of their overall asset size because even if they are unable to raise additional capital, they can make the loans and sell them off. Small banks may still have to raise sufficient liabilities to warehouse the assets until they are securitized and maintain enough equity to offset expected losses on the loans originated. Even so, small banks would be able to originate many more assets than their capital base and overall balance sheet can support and do so without taking undue interest rate risk.

One avenue to achieve that is by networking loan production and selling loans upstream to larger correspondents. The correspondent, in turn, will warehouse the assets until enough volume is accumulated and then securitize and sell them. Upstream securitization is an alternative to outright loan sales and participations.

Credit securitization also offers a method to better diversify credit risk beyond a community bank's target geographic market. It can be used to reduce the credit exposure of the lender to a particular borrower or customer segment. It can also be used as a tool to develop expertise in certain types of loans. The securitization process can be viewed as an extension of the community bank's loan sales network.

Securitization is occurring for many of the same reasons that banks have participated or syndicated loans in the past. It can enhance yields, diversify asset risk both in product mix and geographic location, provide liquidity and funding sources, enhance working relationships with larger banks, and create fee income. As smaller banks experience the competitive pressures of maintaining market share in receivable lending, while non-bank competitors in car loans or credit cards are gaining market share at their expense, securitization can be the solution to the problem.

Where the volume of loans does not merit a one bank securitization program, networking the origination and sale of the product to an upstream warehouse institution provides an alternative for the small banks to enhance their competitive position. This is particularly true for community banks which are much better at generating deposits than originating loans. Those loans that they can generate and that are creditworthy may not offer the spread needed to cover the costs of regulated capital requirements and deposits insurance. Securitization permits these banks to maintain a more efficient capital structure and to replace low margin assets with securitization investments which are higher yielding and more diversified. Poor asset generators can use asset-backed securities to augment their investment portfolios at lower risk-based capital and higher returns.

Securitization has some potential negative impact on banks that make their living off core earnings and net interest margin. Securitization can result in thinner margins between the cost of funds and the yield on assets. When a local institution has little competition in soliciting deposits and loans, it can afford wider spreads. Now that there is national competition on both deposits and loans, the spreads are getting thinner. New competition has been attracted by securitization in two ways. Mortgage bankers now have more outlets for funds than in the past due to the liquidity of securitized loans, and their acceptance by so many new investors, both individuals and institutions. As a result, the competition in the local community for available loans has intensified. As securitization expands beyond the mortgages and consumer paper, the spreads in other markets will shrink as well.

There are additional risks associated with securitization. The process is not completely under the control of the bank that has originated the loans, packaged them, and sold them. The guaranteeing agencies have certain standards that the institution must meet in order to get the credit enhancement that makes the securities packages saleable. The resultant dilemma is that the originator may end up packaging and selling its best loans and keep only the poorer ones in its own portfolio which, in turn, means an increasing overall risk profile of the loan portfolio of the securitizing institution.

We have already identified the capital and funding benefits that securitization offers. It can also be a risk repackaging tool that creates savings for banks in other ways. Securitization lays off credit risk, as just mentioned. At the same time, since the originating bank must provide a first loss guarantee usually in the form of a spread account, it is still going to absorb the credit risk for *expected* losses. The bank will not have to absorb the risk of unexpected losses due to exceptional circumstances. In fact, securitization creates three levels of risk, each of which is borne by the participant best suited to support it. The first level is credit risk for expected losses which is borne by the originator. The second level is concentration risk arising from a lack of diversification, which is borne by the investors. When credit enhancement is available, the catastrophic risk would be spread to the credit enhancer and any residual risk would be borne by the investor.

Should You Be Issuing Asset-Backed Securities?

Asset securitization is not for everyone. You can quickly determine whether or not your institution should explore securitizing some of its assets by answering some simple questions.

1. *Is your institution asset constrained?* Are you growing so quickly that the build-up of loans is straining your working capital and your capital ratios? Are you growing faster than your capital? Do you have capital adequacy constraints? Are your assets not profitable enough, so that you would benefit from getting them off your books and redeploying your assets elsewhere? Do you have an asset/liability management gap problem that you would like resolved?

2. *Are your assets securitizable?* Assets must meet the following three criteria in order to be suitable for securitization:

◆ Predictable and Diversified Risk Characteristics

Although almost any asset can be securitized with some work, the key to smooth asset securitization is the predictability of the risk. That means having a history of delinquency and write-offs that can be used as a guide to future behavior. In addition, greater diversification in the asset base reduces the level of risk and ensures that the pool will not be hit severely by significant loan losses as a result of a single default. Predictable risk can also be achieved using credit enhancement. In addition, predictable duration, if achievable, is helpful, as investors want to know what the prepayment behavior of the security is.

◆ Predictable Payment Stream and Timing

Since most asset-backed securities are pass-throughs, in which case both principal and interest are passed through to the investor when received, investors need to have a reliable idea of the timing of payments. For example, 30-year mortgages have an expected average life of 12 years, four-year car loans have an expected average life of 18 months. The security is priced against the Treasury yield curve and, therefore, the duration of the cash flow is essential for pricing. The less certain the duration, the higher the spread and the more attractive the yield to investors but the higher the cost to the issuing institution. Asset-backed securities with average maturities longer than three years are handled quite differently. These mortgage-backed securities have a set of rules and regulatory handling unique to themselves. However, the market dynamics ultimately work the same.

3. *Do you have the size and ability to generate and support an asset-based security?*

Although the break-even minimum level of an asset-based security should be $75 million, institutions that don't have sufficient volume can pool their resources to recreate a large enough pool to economically generate a security. Market conditions also play a role in making a decision whether to securitize or not. For example, in a flat yield curve market with changing and perhaps falling interest rates, asset-backed securities are not as competitive. This is due to the compression of the yield curve and the fact that interest volatility, particularly with rising rates, will make the price of the asset-backed security more uncertain. Thus, market conditions should always be considered when packaging an asset-backed security.

Funding costs should play a role in making a decision on securitization. Table 8–5 is an example of an analysis of the funding costs and the profit and loss impact of securitization, both public and private, versus internal funding.

Cost-Benefit Analysis

Performing the cost-benefit analysis of securitizing a package of financial assets involves, at minimum, *analysis of the funding costs of the different securitizing alternatives versus internal funding.* Table 8–5 displays the funding costs for three alternatives; internal funding, private placement securitization, and public securitization by an A-rated bank. As Table 8–5 indicates, securitization can save between 150 and 175 basis points of funding costs to the issuing institution. The credit enhancement costs when calculated in basis points over the total portfolio are not as high as may appear. In general, letters of credit or surety bonds cover a percentage of the principal, usually between 7 percent and 12 percent. That actual percentage reflects the risk characteristics of the portfolio. The fees for credit enhancements range from 75 to 150 basis points. In this particular case, a letter of credit for 9 percent of the total portfolio ($27 million) was to be issued with a 50 basis point fee for a cost of 4.5 basis points per year. This letter of credit would cover all scheduled principal and interest payments so long as delinquencies and losses do not exceed 9 percent of the portfolio. This appears to be sufficient coverage since historically losses ranged around 50 basis points and delinquencies around 150 basis points.

Table 8–5: Funding Costs for an AAA-Backed Security by an A-Rated Bank

	Public Issue	Private Placement	Internal Funding
1. Three-year Treasury	9.10%	9.10%	
2. Spread over Treasury (basis points)	60-85	70-105	debt costs
3. Total yield to investor	9.70%-9.95%	9.80%-10.15%	9.90%-10.10%
4. Credit enhancement (basis points)	3-6	3-6	—
5. Underwriting fees (based on $1 million to $1.5 million annualized) (basis points)	12-17	12-17	—
6. Printing, legal, blue sky fee (basis points)	7-10	4-6	—
7. Annual costs (basis points)	2-3	1-2	equity costs
8. Total issue costs (basis points)	24-36	20-31	—
9. Average cost (annualized)	9.94%-10.31%	10.00%-10.46%	11.42%-12.09%[†]
10. First year average cost	10.42%-10.92%	10.32%-10.82%	WACC*

Source: John W. Ballantine, Jr., "Should Your Bank be Issuing Asset-backed Securities?" *Bank Accounting and Finance*

[†]Assumes 100% equity capitalization and pretax ROE between 25% and 30%
*WAAC: weighted average cost of capital

The issue coupon is expressed as a spread over Treasuries, the extent of the spread depends upon market conditions, the type of collateral offered for securitization (cars, computers, airplanes, etc.), the liquidity of the paper and its rating. The private placement market usually demands a liquidity premium of 10 to 20 basis points.

Underwriting fees range between 40 and 100 basis points. Fees are determined based upon the relationship between the investment banker and the issuer as well as the frequency of issuing, the complexity of each issue, and the size of each transaction. Printing, legal, and prospectus fees for a publicly issued security are significantly higher than those for a private placement.

Annual costs, which include reporting, accounting, and other costs, are often higher for public issues than for private placements. Total issue costs ranged here between 20 and 35 basis points of the security for a $300 million issue. Costs will increase as a percent of the total issue as the asset size of the security declines. This is a clear case of economies of scale where pooling assets across banks may be necessary to create sufficient size for economies of scale.

Cost comparisons include average issue costs compared to the weighted average cost of internal funding, which includes the weighted average cost of debt and the pre-tax cost of equity. We assumed here the cost of debt was a three-year debt cost for an A-rated company with a 90 percent debt to equity ratio. The pre-tax cost of equity was based upon an after-tax target return on equity of 15 percent.

The profit and loss and return on equity statement strongly support the funding analysis in making a compelling argument for securitization. It also highlights the trade-offs involved in growth versus slow growth market. Table 8–6 compares internal funding to securitization in the form of pro forma financial statements that would result from issuing a $300 million asset-backed security. With the exception of funding costs, servicing costs of the security versus a normal

Table 8–6: Internal Funding Compared to Issuing an Asset-Backed Security: Net Interest Margin

	Company with Portfolio	Asset-Backed Security
Gross yield	14.0%	14.0%
Funding costs (annual)	(9.9%)	(10.0%-10.3%)
Operating costs	(1.5%)	(1.5%)
Loss reserve	(0.5%)	(0.5%)
Overhead	(1.0%)	(1.0%)
Total costs	(12.9%)	(13.0%-13.3%)
Net margin	1.1%	1.0%-0.7%

Source: John W. Ballantine, Jr., "Should Your Bank be Issuing Asset-backed Securities?" *Bank Accounting and Finance*

loan portfolio are identical when you construct the profit and loss statement. It is difficult, yet important, to have as accurate an estimate as possible for servicing costs, other operating costs, and overhead. These have a significant effect on your net interest margin. The Profit & Loss statement shows that the net interest margin on the portfolio is 20 to 50 basis points higher than the net interest margin on the asset-backed security, which reflects the annualized costs of issuing the security.

Thus, for a company that is not growing and is not facing capital issues, keeping the financial assets on the books and realizing a higher spread may be a better strategy than securitizing them. The trade-off financial institutions face is that although marginal funding costs on asset-backed securities may be less than internal funding costs, profits will also be less, due to other securitization costs.

As profitability is analyzed in terms of return on equity, the picture changes (Table 8–7). Asset securitization does not require equity; in fact, the asset is taken off the books, thereby freeing up some equity for other uses. The return on equity on the asset-backed security is three to four times greater than that of the portfolio lender. The equity required to support the asset-backed security is very small because only a very small portion of the security is actually being carried on the books of the servicing bank/the issuer. Typically 3 percent to 4 percent of the asset being serviced are on the books.

The critical assumption in calculating return on equity is that the asset-backed security is accounted for as a sale without recourse. If any recourse, even limited,

Table 8–7: Internal Funding Compared to Issuing an Asset-Backed Security: Return on Equity (thousands of dollars)

	Company with Portfolio	Asset-Backed Security
Net margin	1.1%	1.0%-0.7%
Profit before tax	$3,300	$3,000-$2,100
Net profit after tax (40% tax rate)	$1,980	$1,800-$1,260
Equity required	$21,000-$30,000	$4,000-$5,000
Return on equity	6.6%-9.4%	25%-36%

Source: John W. Ballantine, Jr., "Should Your Bank be Issuing Asset-backed Securities?" *Bank Accounting and Finance*

is an integral part of the sale, then additional equity is required which, in turn, will change the returns.

In this example, we did not consider asset-backed securities as an asset/liability management tool. We looked at them as a way to mitigate capital constraints and facilitate redeployment of capital and growth opportunities.

Mortgage Securitization

Since the first mortgage-backed security (MBS) was issued by the Government National Mortgage Association in 1970, the market has exploded. Today the MBS market is over $900 billion, up from $112 billion in 1980. By the end of the decade, experts say, the figure could easily top $2 trillion. The largest issuers of mortgage-backed securities are the Government National Mortgage Association (Ginnie Mae), the Federal National Mortgage Association (Fannie Mae) and the Federal Home Loan Mortgage Corporation (Freddie Mac). The mortgage securities issued by the three agencies are packaged pools of mortgages that are sold as bonds. All mortgages are given rates that fall within the 100 to 200 basis point range. The securities are pass-throughs, in other words the investor receives monthly a pro rata share of regular interest and principal payments as well as any unscheduled prepayments on the mortgages. Mortgage-backed securities of all forms, including collateralized mortgage obligations (CMOs), real estate mortgage investment conduits (REMICs), and interest only/principal-only securities (IO/POs), have become an important investment vehicle in the 1990s. A demand for securities-backed U.S. home mortgages has skyrocketed and is approaching the $1 trillion mark.

In this book we are not looking at mortgage-backed securities as an investment vehicle, instead we look at them as a balance sheet management tool in the same sense that other asset securitizations were described earlier. They have the same benefits and disadvantages associated with other types of asset securitization with few exceptions. The depths of the mortgage-backed securities market is much greater than any other asset pool. The market is much more liquid and is institutionalized through the quasi-government agencies. Since the market is more mature than other asset securitization forms, issuance costs and liquidity considerations are more preferential than other asset-based securities. Further, banks and thrifts can now originate fixed-rate or variable-rate mortgages as well, because the option of securitizing the mortgages and selling them off the balance is readily available. As a result, asset/liability management considerations are less important. This provides a great relief to the thrift industry in particular and to consumers who seek fixed-rate mortgages because it is the interest rate risk that the thrift industry assumed in the late 1970s and 1980s that was at the root of its demise. That interest rate risk directly related to fixed-rate assets, which were funded by shorter term or variable-rate liabilities. Mortgage securitization eliminates that risk in balance sheet management.

Mortgage-Backed Securities

There are several kinds of mortgage-backed securities which involve home mortgages. These include the following:

1. *Traditional Fixed-Rate Mortgage-Backed Securities.* These pass-throughs have sufficient drawbacks for some investors to impair their marketability. These securities do not have a fixed maturity date when all principal is repaid. As a reflection of the underlying pool of mortgages, each monthly payment includes interest and principal that are necessary to amortize the underlying loans. However, when prepayments occur, these are passed through to the investor as well.

Prepayments are a major issue in securitization and the pricing of mortgage-backed securities. The rate of prepayments is typically inversely related to the direction of interest rates. Prepayments accelerate when interest rates drop, which reflects the tendency of homeowners to refinance existing mortgages or buy new homes. The higher prepayment rate curtails the life of an MBS which, in turn, means that the investor must search for a new investment much sooner than originally anticipated and because interest rates are falling, comparable investments have a lower yield. This is the reinvestment risk associated with prepayments of mortgage-backed securities.

For the issuer, changes in mortgage prepayment rates can also cause significant interest rate risk problems on the balance sheet. When interest rates are rising, prepayments usually decline, which means that a longer effective life for the security with below market rate returns. If that long-term asset is financed by short-term money, the negative gap will cause significant losses. This is what happened to the thrifts in the early 1980s. Betting on the timing and direction of interest rates and ignoring the impact of interest rate risk is diametrically opposed to the hedging concept and to the thesis on which this book is based. As a result, straight pass-throughs have major shortcomings as an interest rate management tool for an issuing bank.

2. *CMOs and REMICs*. CMOs were introduced in the early 1980s as a tool to reduce both reinvestment and interest rate risks that were associated with the standard MBS investments. CMOs slice the cash flows from the traditional MBS into tranches of various maturities. These maturities will match the maturity and cash flow needs of a variety of different issuers and investors. The need for even greater flexibility in the mortgage security structure created the REMICs. The issuance of REMICs contributed to the explosion of mortgage-backed securities.

Today almost all CMOs or multiple-class securities are issued in REMIC form. Most come from Fannie Mae and Freddie Mac, which, together issued $98 billion of REMICs in 1990. The role of the government agencies as intermediaries and market makers significantly increased the depth of the secondary mortgage market and provided liquidity and balance sheet flexibility in mortgage management never before available.

By pooling different components of the cash flow from underlying standard mortgage-backed securities (MBS), issuers can create tranches with fully customized interest rates, average coupons, and final maturities. A REMIC may include any number of classes of regular interests. These tranches are often labelled as A, B, or C class. They are assigned fixed, floating, or zero interest rate, a fixed principal amount and all kinds of payment conditions. Often one or more Z classes similar to a zero coupon or accrual bond are included as regular interest classes. In addition, there is a single class of residual interest typically called the R class, which can be structured in any number of ways. The R class generally receives the remaining cash flow from the MBS which is not distributed to the regular class.

A variation on the REMIC structure involves sequential disbursements. In these cases, principal-only regular classes are usually returned sequentially in alphabetical order to the investors. All the investors in the regular class except principal-only and accrual or Z classes are paid interest currently on their pro rata share of the remaining principal. Principal payments to individual tranches do not start until previous tranches are retired. Only the A tranch initially is repaying principal. After the A tranches repaid in full the B tranch begins repaying principal and so on and so on.

The final regular class of a REMIC often is an accrual class or Z tranch. It receives no interest payments until certain other classes have paid down. Instead, interest accrues and the balance of the tranch grows at the coupon interest rate compounded monthly until all other priority classes have been retired. At that time the Z tranch converts to an ordinary interest paying mortgage security that pays principal monthly until it is fully amortized.

The weighted average life and yield of the different tranches vary greatly. The credit risk is minimal because REMICs issued by Fannie Mae or Freddie Mac are backed by a collateral that is guaranteed by government agencies. There is no event risk which does apply in corporate bonds, whereby the securities will suffer a market loss as a result of an unforeseen event that will negatively impact the issuers credit rating. In addition, risk-based capital guidelines issued by bank and thrift regulatory agencies extend preferential capital treatment to most regular interest REMIC tranches.

There are many more complex REMIC structures, including a planned amortization class (PAC) issue, targeted amortization class (TAC) issue, floating rate tranches, and interest only or principal only tranches. The variations are potentially infinite. These variations permit issuing REMIC structures with more predictable cash flows. TAC tranches, for example, increase the predictability of cash flows, while other tranches are less predictable and may be useful to investors with an overall asset/liability management strategy or total return investment strategy. Structures with highly volatile cash flows are yield enhancers to overall portfolio management. Other structures, such as IO and PO tranches, may be extremely sensitive to prepayments. Material negative effects on yield and on initial investment recouping are fully disclosed in the prospectus supplement of each REMIC issue. There are also important tax considerations and financial accounting considerations which need to be taken into account.

The securitization of mortgages has created an overflow into commercial mortgage securitization. The tremendous volume of commercial mortgages that is coming to the market from the RTC and the emergence of conduit programs may increase the liquidity and depth of the commercial mortgage securitization market significantly, although currently the market is thin and investor interest is insufficient to expect securitization to become commonplace. Without investors, securitization is not going to happen because liquidity is the key to the success of the market.

The formation of commercial mortgage conduits fills the void left by undercapitalized thrifts, retreating banks, and insurance companies. Conduit programs have been successfully implemented in the single family mortgage-backed security market, but to date have only been contemplated in commercial mortgage securitization. Applications of private placements and other programs have been quite limited. The originators of commercial mortgages have retreated from the market in recent years. A solid network of banks and thrifts that originate commercial mortgages is essential to structure the market in a way that will provide sufficient diversity of mortgages to create less risky mortgage pools. The originators, of course, will benefit from securitization programs because they will be able to service their existing customer base, roll over existing loans if they do not meet underwriting guidelines, generate origination and servicing income and keep the loan off their balance sheets. The benefits of other securitization programs apply here as well. However, the mechanics of a conduit program are not in place and commercial mortgages as well as small business loans are way behind in the securitization game.

The success of the government agency programs in residential mortgage securitization encouraged private sector institutions to securitize mortgage debt themselves. These new securities are patterned after the government ones but offer more flexibility and the opportunity to package nonconforming loans. The government agencies cannot buy, sell or trade single family mortgages with balances exceeding $133,250. Larger mortgages do not conform with government requirements. 25 percent of the total dollar value of mortgages, virtually one in seven mortgages, are comprised of nonconforming loans. During the 1980s, the secondary market has come into its own. In 1970, 39 percent of single family originations were sold into the secondary market. By 1985, 80 percent of single-family originations were securitized. Economic conditions, interest rates, regulatory changes and market dynamics have all provided impetus to the creation of new types of mortgages and the securities which are backed by them.

The proliferation of mortgage-backed securities reflects the creativity of the investment community as well as the need to tailor new instruments to attract new investor dollars and to better meet asset/liability management needs. Much like the explosion of derivative types in the swaps, options and futures markets asset securitization is seeing new esoteric securities created each and every day. As consumer demand for mortgage credit is increasing, securitization becomes an attractive alternative to meeting their needs without incurring interest rate risk or without warehousing the assets to a point where capital ratios are being stretched.

Mortgages are comprised of two components, the actual liability and the servicing annuity. Earnings are generated both by interest on the mortgage and/or by the servicing fee. These are two completely separate assets, each commanding a market price and each being tradeable to different buyers. A bank that wishes to issue a mortgage-backed security needs to form a pool large enough for the security. The bank, therefore, may need to approach other lenders in order to buy additional loans to create a pool large enough to be securitized. A primary lender may agree to sell a pool of mortgages to the issuing bank and demand to retain the primary servicing. In return, the issuing bank will pay the primary lender/servicer a service fee for sending notices to homeowners and collecting payments.

If, for example, the coupon of the mortgages was 10 percent and the service fee is 40 basis points the net pass-through rate to the issuer bank is 9.6 percent. As the issuer bank continues to purchase loans from several primary lenders, a master servicer needs to be created since different pools within the master pool are serviced by different originators. Typically, the issuer bank functions as the master servicer. It collects the payments from the primary servicers, aggregates them, and returns a single payment to the investor. Master servicing has a cost of its own which runs from 25 to 50 basis points. The net rate to the investor in this example is 9.1 percent.

What does an issuer need to do in order to securitize the pool of loans? Credit enhancement is the first step. The credit enhancement in the form of an insurance policy or a back-up letter of credit normally covers only the 5 percent to 10 percent of the pool's value, much like in other securitization activities. The credit enhancement is an essential stop-loss provision required by the rating agencies. In addition, special hazard insurance and bankruptcy insurance must be provided by the issuer. A certain amount of underwriting is also required. The payment history of the borrowers needs to be investigated as well as the current value of the property, a certification by FHA or VA or private mortgage insurance, the existence of enforceable notes or a deed, title opinion and title insurance and so on.

The different responsibilities of the issuers are best illustrated through an example of a default situation. Take an original mortgage given on a $100,000 property for $85,000. Primary mortgage insurance would be required, possibly as low as $75,000. Five years later the borrowers default. There is an $80,000 outstanding balance on the loan. The primary servicer will first sell the property. Given the decline in real estate values he or she realizes only $60,000. The next recourse is the primary mortgage insurance. The primary servicer files a $10,000 claim representing the full amount of coverage purchased. Now the issuer has recouped $70,000. If the loan was sold as a part of a mortgage-backed security, part of the issuer's credit enhancement would cover the remaining $10,000 in this example. The issuer/master servicer will pay that amount. At the end of the day the investor is not negatively affected. Generally, the issuer limits its coverage to 10 percent of the overall pool size betting that properties will escalate in value, that the underwriting was good and that the mortgages will not go into default.

The advantages of securitization for the issuer are many. Securitization provides a liquidity to an otherwise illiquid asset. A bank can sell the asset and reinvest the cash in order to properly balance the asset/liability management position from a maturity standpoint. Further, as a result of redeploying the assets for mortgages into government securities, they carry no bad-debt provision and lower risk-based capital requirements. From the investor's standpoint, there are many advantages as well. However, we are looking at the transaction from the hedger/issuer standpoint, although many banks are major investors in the mortgage-backed securities as well. As an issuer, a bank can swap its mortgages for an enhanced asset.

For instance, if a bank holds $100 million worth of seasoned mortgages, it can sell this mature portfolio to the issuer at market or at a premium (thereby booking instant gain and, therefore, increased retained earnings) and get in return a security which will be backed by the bank's mortgages. If the bank retains the security instead of cash, it does not have to realize a book loss, according to generally accepted accounting principles, if the mortgages were under water and the securities were sold at a discount. The reason is the bank is getting back a like asset. It is really the same asset but it is enhanced because the credit risk has been transferred to the issuer.

There are three options for a private issue: a registered rated security, a registered unrated security, or a private placement. The parameters vary, but the general rule is the tighter the restrictions, the higher the price you will receive. If the loans are conforming loans, agency pass-through programs provide the most cost effective outlet. Ginnie Mae packages current mortgages including mortgages pooled within a year of issuance. Fannie Mae securitizes both new and seasoned pools. It focuses primarily on fixed-rate mortgages that have been outstanding for one or more years. Freddie Mac products are similar. Since government agency issues are deemed to be of the highest quality, they are generally not rated by the independent agencies. The thrift side of this benefit is that agency securities are very strict. Often a third or more of the loans in an average mature portfolio will not meet their criteria. Private issues are more flexible and have generally been comprised of nonconforming loans.

Credit enhancement is not necessary for private mortgage pass-throughs. The rating agencies will provide a rating based upon the type of property, the type of mortgage, the underwriting standards, maturity, and geographic dispersement, as well as internal pool characteristics including diversification. A rated security will, of course, command a higher price, but it may be too restrictive and the issuer must comply with the rating agencies' criteria, which means the need for quality credit enhancement as well as special hazard and bankruptcy insurance. Sometimes these are hard to come by. For example, it is nearly impossible to get special hazard insurance today on mortgages held in California. A private placement or an unrated security allows the issuer to skip some of those requirements as well as SEC registrations in the event of a private placement. Flexibility and price are directly related in this case. The greater the flexibility, the higher the price.

There are several alternatives available to the pool structure. The variables include:

◆ Differing versus same rates

◆ Differing versus same maturities

Each security is given a coupon or a pass-through rate, a pool issue date, a maturity date, and a payment delay period. In many cases, a weighted average coupon (WAC) is needed, since the underlying mortgages have different interest rates. The WAC equals the weighed average of the underlying mortgage interest rates as of the pool issue date, using the balance of each mortgage as the weighting factor. The disadvantage of a security structured in this way is that the prepayment rates vary, which in turn causes it to trade at lower prices.

Another structuring alternative is to cluster mortgage coupons in 1 percent to 2 percent ranges to construct separate subseries of different coupons. Each will be priced to market separately. The pool issue date is the date of issuing the security, not the date of issue of the underlying mortgage. The maturity date is the date of the latest maturing underlying mortgage. Even if 99 percent of the mortgages in the pool mature in 15 years, that 1 percent that matures in 30 years will create an overall pool maturity of 30 years. A weighted average maturity (WAM) is also figured to clarify the cash flows and yields. This is the weighted average of the remaining term of all the underlying mortgages as of issue date. The balance of each mortgage is the weighting factor.

Another factor to be taken into account is the payment delay period. That refers to the time lag between the date the homeowners are scheduled to make their mortgage payments and the date the servicing institution pays the pool investor. The payment delay varies greatly depending upon the type of pass-through. It could be fifty, sixty, seventy days. The longer the payment delay, the less the yield to the investor.

Hold the Security or Sell the Cash

There are different considerations that enter the decision whether to hold the security once the loan pool has been securitized or to sell it off altogether for cash. Holding the security reduces the bad debt provision. The assets will move from a loan category to an investment category in the balance sheet. There are other disadvantages to selling the assets altogether if the pool is sold at a discount. In these situations, the bank would realize a book loss equal to the discount. However, if the bank runs the loss against its tax return, the loss could cut taxes significantly. The bank can carry back losses for ten years. If a bank has a tax liability, the book loss can be applied to generate a refund.

Residential mortgages are ideal securitization candidates. Their small size creates significant risk diversification, whereas with a commercial portfolio that diversification is much smaller. To create $100 million security, for example, it may take only ten commercial mortgages but it could take one to two thousand residential mortgages. When size is concerned, however, car loans and credit card lines might include even more individual loans, often five times as many as mortgages. That, in turn, requires much more costly paperwork to assemble. Securitization is not a free ride. There is significant cost involved including legal fees and SEC charges. On a $100 million pool, the SEC charges will be $20,000, legal fees could range in the $50,000 range, accounting costs at $20,000 and printing at $35,000; add in $35,000 for filing of assignments and the total comes to $160,000. For a long-term the annual costs are pretty low, but for a portfolio with a WAC of eighteen months or a very small portfolio that contains less than $25 million in assets, securitization does not make sense. The costs will then outweigh the benefits. Consequently, residential mortgages, car loans, credit term assets can all be securitized. However, short-term notes, volatile credit, commercial loans and the like are unlikely securitization candidates.

Conclusion

Securitization revolutionized the asset side of the thrift's balance sheet. It created the flexibility of removing undesirable assets of the balance sheets, thereby increasing the thrift's flexibility to manage a broad range of assets such as capital, fee income, and interest rate risk. Securitization is available for all types of assets, including residential mortgages and other consumer loans.

The breadth of asset types and securities instruments available to thrifts today has changed the fundamentals of the business. Thrifts can now originate assets which they do not intend to hold for portfolio. That capability is important in meeting further needs which do not fit the thrift's risk profile or other strategic considerations. It also helps generate fee income by using the balance sheet to warehouse loans and then sell them, retaining the original fees and securitization gains. In summary, securitization is an important tool which thrifts can use to achieve their strategic objectives and retain their business focus within the paperwork of their mixed parameters and capital depth.

The Tool Box

9

Identifying Your Strategic Niche: The Use of Strategic Planning Tools

Definition of Strategic Planning

Strategic planning is a systematic approach to the management of change. It is a process that can be used to approach an uncertain future in an organized manner. Thus, planning is not a process distinct from management but a vital and important activity which should become an integral part of management. As each thrift executive struggles with reassessing the identify of his other institution, planning becomes an essential tool for that assessment process. Planning involves assessment of the current situation, decisions regarding future objectives or direction, and development and implementation of actions to achieve stated objectives. In essence, strategic planning provides answers to the following questions:

◆ Where am I now?

◆ Who am I and who do I want to be?

◆ Where do I want to be?

◆ How do I get there?

These questions are answered every day as management makes personnel or staffing decisions, puts new policies or procedures into place, or goes after a potential new customer. If such questions are not answered explicitly from a long-term perspective, the answer may be produced by the cumulative impact of day-to-day or month-to-month decisions. Many management decisions, each made with a short-term perspective, constitute one approach to managing change. However, this approach is not adequate for addressing sudden, turbulent change. In addition, it ignores future threats and opportunities until they become present events, when it may be too late to fully capitalize on or avoid them Thus, this approach may not contribute to long-term success and profitability.

A long-term approach to managing change has become a necessity for thrifts. Few industries have experienced the turbulent changes now taking place in the financial services industry. The symptoms of these changes are widely publicized and were discussed earlier in the book.

The accelerating pace of change in the financial services industry, coupled with tremendous uncertainty about the future, have increased the need for bank management to have the ability to react to rapid change in a constructive, thoughtful manner. In fact, the ability to react and adapt successfully has become a prime determinant of the winners and losers in the new financial services industry. This new environment demands that future opportunities be identified, explored, and, if appropriate, developed in a thorough and systematic manner. Strategic planning offers the process and methodology to assist bankers with such responsibilities. As the thrift industry searches for new strategic identity, the process of strategic planning becomes integral to that quest, a critical tool in determining what the institution's future will be.

Strategic Planning Overview

Strategic planning is not, as some banks practice it, an exercise in budgeting or preparing detailed financial or economic models. It is a process, a continuing analysis of existing and potential markets, products and competitors. The results of this analysis translate into a set of objectives and strategies to realize these objectives. With strategies defined, the resources of the bank can be systematically applied on a day-to-day and long-term basis (see Figure 9–1). Strategic planning is

Figure 9-1: The Logical Flow of the Strategic Planning Process

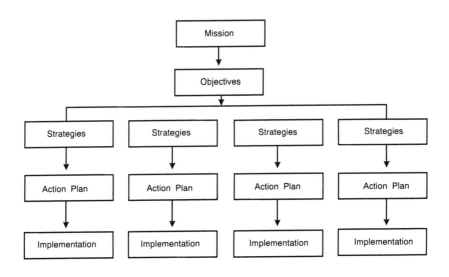

specifically geared to increase a bank's flexibility, its ability to change, and its capacity for generating new and creative options. However, all banks differ in some respects, so it follows that not all planning systems are or should be identical. There is no "ideal" strategic planning system for every bank. Strategic planning systems must be designed to fit the unique characteristics of each organization. Nevertheless, there are common elements among planning systems, which can be identified and tailored to form a planning system for a particular institution. The purpose of this chapter is to briefly explain these common elements and present an overview of the process. Subsequent chapters provide specific techniques and suggestions to effectively use strategic planning to identify the right strategic option for your thrift.

The Framework for Strategic Planning

The logic of planning process is fairly straightforward. The bank's mission or purpose is described, objectives are defined, its environment is analyzed, and strategies are developed to realize objectives. These strategies are then translated into specific action plans and implementation programs. Finally implementation is monitored and evaluated to ensure effective implementation and to provide feedback into the process as the planning cycle is repeated. The planning process, then is an ongoing and flexible process. It does not end in the production of a paper document, but rather continues through implementation and continuous update.

In the following pages, the general components of the strategic planning process are described. They components are:

◆ The Plan to Plan

◆ The Mission and Objectives

◆ Situation Assessment

◆ Strategy Development and Selection

◆ Action Plans for Implementation

◆ Monitoring and Evaluation

These aspects of the strategic planning process are arranged in approximate chronological order with each step providing the basis for subsequent steps.

The Plan to Plan

The Plan to Plan is a brief document outlining the basic steps in the planning process. It typically begins as a conceptual model of the process; as the practical aspects of the planning cycle are flushed out, it becomes an operational overview.

The plan outlines the schedule, milestones and methodology for developing and updating the strategic plans. The plan also identifies which individuals will participate in the strategic planning process and delineates responsibility for completion of certain products and tasks. The plan also includes highlights of the bank-level situation assessment which provide the data base for the planning units to commence their plan development.

The Mission and Objectives

The mission statement described the bank's overall purpose (see Figure 9–2). This statement "sets the stage" for the strategic planning process and expresses the beliefs of the chief executive and senior management. The mission statement forms the premise against which objectives and strategic decision making are developed. The mission statement also answers the question, "What kind of thrift or a financial services company do we want to become?" For example, a thrift may revise its mission statement from a real estate focused company to a community banking, full-service company. Or, the change may represent an extension of the business from residential real estate lending to lending and securitization, toward the creation of a mortgage banking company.

Objectives described where the bank wants to be and provide for a more specific, implementation-oriented "translation" of the mission. Objectives may be either qualitative (e.g., serve the community) or quantitative (e.g., 1 percent ROA), and will typically elaborate on the more general and sweeping statements that

Figure 9–2: Strategic Planning Components

Mission	Who are we?
Objectives	Where do we want to go?
Strategies	How do we get there?
Implementation	Converting the plan into reality.

compromise the bank mission statement. Objectives should be set for those aspects of the bank for which plans will be created. Without objectives, bank resources and talent may lack direction, focus, and consistency. For example, if a shift in focus is contemplated, a reasonable objective may be a change in business mix, such as from 80 percent mortgages and 20 percent securities to 60 percent mortgages, 30 percent consumer loans and 10 percent securities. Or, from 100 percent consumer oriented to 80 percent consumer and 20 percent small business mix.

Situation Assessment

The situation assessment involves a review of "where the bank is now." It is an analysis of data—past, present, and future—that provides the basis for making decisions. Key trends, forces, and events that have impact on the achievement of the corporate mission and objectives, and hence formulation and implementation of strategies, are identified and analyzed. Changes in the environment have a profound impact on every thrift, and performance will be improved if these changes are identified and anticipated before the impact is felt, or at minimum, contingency plans made. A bank operates within an environment, not a vacuum, and therefore must interact with that environment. Planning that interaction requires information on the environment where actions are to be taken and profits made.

A situation analysis usually involves an external assessment of a bank's environment, including present and potential markets, competitors, the economic and regulatory climate; and an internal analysis of the bank's strengths, weaknesses and capabilities (see Figure 9–3).

Expectations of Major Interests. Since no organization, however large, can examine every factor relevant to strategic decision making, the first step in the situation analysis is identifying what key players are most significant to the achievement of the corporate mission. These elements, which may be either internal or external interests, constitute constraints within which the organization operates.

External factors include the many individuals and groups outside the bank that have a major interest in the impact on the bank's operations and profitability. Hence, their views should be taken into account in the strategic planning process. Examples of such groups include stockholders, consumers, interest groups and the government. Bearing in mind the socioeconomic responsibilities of the bank, these groups can be identified, analyzed, and ranked in importance and impact. An example of such an issue is the "politicizing" of economic/financial decision making—the growing government involvement in bank decisions through consumerism, environmentalism, inflation control, antitrust and, particularly in consumer

Figure 9-3: Situation Analysis

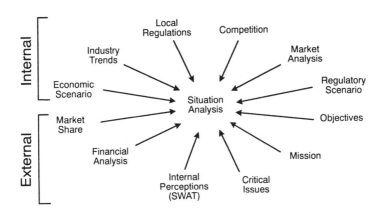

lending, discrimination issues in mortgage lending, regulation pertaining to credit information gathering, truth-in-lending disclosures, and the like.

The regulatory environment is another critical outside factor which has overwhelming impact on the future direction and available strategic alternatives to the business.

The expectations of people inside the bank (not only top management) also represent significant input into the strategic planning process. This is especially true of banks where management is highly sensitive to the interests and values people in the organization. The views of top management, and the board and the CEO in particular, must be taken into account in strategic decisions at all levels. The CEO's views of the bank's mission, ethical standards, target markets, performance expectations, and critical issues are basic premises in the strategic planning process.

Creating a database containing information about past performance, the current situation, and the future is another important step in strategic planning, which is a data-based activity. The types of information usually collected include the following:

♦ Financial information (profitability, efficiency, growth)

♦ Market information (market share, segments, growth, prospective analysis, market needs)

♦ Economic projections

♦ Regulations scenario

♦ Competition (share, dominance, strategies)

♦ Image

This information can be used to identify and evaluate alternative courses of action.

Data about past performance is also useful for educating those not intimately familiar with a particular product or division, and as a basis for assessing the present situation and possible future developments. If, for example, market share in a particular segment has been declining for the past five years and that segment has been a prime target market, then current performance is not satisfactory and should be more closely investigated. Reasons for failure, (e.g., declining market, competition dominance, or ineffective entry techniques), should be identified. Furthermore, any projected rise in market share must be thoroughly justified in light of this trend.

Information collected about the current situation should include items that management perceives as important. These factors and the depth of the analysis performed will vary by bank.

Data about the future traditionally involves projections of future economic trends. However, today's complex environment in which the banking industry operates requires more than economic trends and financial projections of revenues, profits and market share. Each bank should identify specific factors to forecast, including technological developments, social changes (e.g., changing social values), risk forecasts, and legislative/regulatory changes. The data base and the external expectations information provide the inputs into the analysis of a bank's strengths, weaknesses, opportunities and threats.

Strategy Development and Selection

Internal contemplation and full understanding of the company's true strengths, weaknesses, opportunities, and threats is key to the success of any strategic initiative. It is difficult to take a candid view of the company and accept the weaknesses along with the strengths. It is, however, most important to develop an understanding of the true reality of the institution. Management weakness, for example, will make the likelihood of success of any strategic position low, since management of the bank and its subsidiaries is a difficult yet pivotal element to any strategy's success. Low service levels make community banking a more difficult strategy to implement, although such weakness can be fully corrected. Or, weakness in the origination network may imply the absence of any competitive advantage to the thrift in entering mortgage banking and securitization operations.

Each one of these weaknesses can be addressed. However, a realistic view of the company is essential to coming to grips with such weaknesses and to selecting the strategic position with the highest likelihood of success.

Data gathering can be overbearing. Strategic planning is an activity which deals with unknowns and with the future. The plan represents management's best guess as to the direction which will most likely bring future success and realize the company's mission. At the same time, no amount of data gathering can predict the future with certainty. Consequently, although strategic planning is indeed a data-based activity, it is important to put that component in perspective, and not to reach paralysis by overanalysis.

Strategic planning is a creative process and, although it needs information as its basis, it is ultimately management acumen and creative thinking which determine the future direction of the thrift.

Analysis of the external and internal environment leads to the identification of strategies that the bank should undertake. Many techniques have been developed to perform these analyses. Three approaches which may be useful include: market attractiveness/business position analysis, critical issues analysis, and WOTS-Up analysis (Weaknesses, Opportunities, Threats, and Strengths).

The market attractiveness/business position analysis technique combines external and internal analyses relating business position to particular markets. This is accomplished by preparing a list of all relevant market factors and assessing both the attractiveness of the market and the strength of your performance in it with respect to these factors. The results, arrayed on a market by market basis, identify potential opportunities and structure market entry and product development strategies accordingly.

Action Plans for Implementation

Without implementation, the strategic planning process is rendered moot. In order to assure implementation, action plans must be developed which lay out the steps needed to convert the plan into reality. These action plans specify operating objectives and specific activities required to implement strategies. An effective action plan will include a task description, a schedule or timetable, resource requirements, a budget, decision points, and performance standards for measuring task completion and success.

Monitoring and Evaluation

The monitoring and evaluation stage is intended to measure progress toward attaining the objectives developed in previous stages. Criteria for measuring the success of the strategic planning effort should be established to allow management to evaluate and improve strategy development in future planning cycles. In this way, problems with the process can be ameliorated, ineffective strategies eliminated, and a basis for improving the process during the next planning cycle developed. Common problems associated with the planning process are described in the next section.

Common Pitfalls—Why Planning Fails

There are numerous reasons why planning fails. Because strategic planning is an integral part of management, the reasons for failure may be as many and varied as the reasons for bad management. However, there appears to be some consistency about the nature of failure. Strategic planning efforts are unsuccessful if

- ◆ A strategic plan is developed but never used

- ◆ Inappropriate methodology or insufficient data is available for developing strategies

- ◆ The planning effort results in inappropriate or ill-advised strategies

- ◆ Any combination of the above

The reasons for failure can include the following:

Lack of Commitment by Top Management. Top management must endorse the planning process by participation in the development of the plan and providing commitment to the plan once it is in place. Without such commitment, the rest of the bank will not attach high priority to strategic planning.

Excessive Delegation. If the planning process is delegated to the planning staff without sufficient involvement by top management, plan implementation will not be viewed as a high priority activity.

Vagueness. Goals, objectives, strategies and action plans should be specific and measurable. It is not always easy to develop and obtain commitment to specific goals. With measurable goals comes the possibility for failure and risk adverse managers are unlikely to commit to goal setting or the process.

Inadequate Input. Strategies should be based on accurate data on the bank environment. Reasoned judgments and effective strategies are less likely to be developed with good data.

Crisis Orientation. Over committed management facing daily crises will not have sufficient time for the reflection required by strategic planning.

"Trying to Do Too Much." In developing a strategic plan, management should remember that major changes in direction require time and acceptance by those affected.

Failure to Bring Line Management into the Strategic Planning Process. These are the individuals who are responsible for implementing the strategic plan. Without a sense of involvement or "ownership," plan goals have less chance of being realized.

There are a myriad of other reasons why strategic planning fails. In embarking on the development of a strategic plan, it may be useful to identify potential reasons for failure and thus avoid the many obstacles and impediments to a successful plan.

Glossary

The following glossary defines the critical elements of the strategic planning process.

Action Plans. A program for implementing a strategy. An action plan describes tasks to be completed, timing, project responsibilities, resource requirements, expected benefits, and key decision points.

Critical Issues Approach. A process by which important strategic issues are identified. Strategies are developed to address each critical issue.

Growth Share Matrix. A matrix for describing the market share and market growth rate potential for Strategic Business Units (SBUs). It suggests strategies depending upon the SBU's position.

Market Attractiveness/Business Positioning Attractiveness Matrix. A matrix for describing the relationship between market potential and the bank's position in that market.

Market Segmentation. A technique to find groups within current and potential markets with homogeneous needs and characteristics.

Mission Statement. A concise, general statement describing what kind of an institution the bank is and wants to be.

Objectives. Specific qualitative and quantitative statements describing where the bank wants to go, i.e., what needs to be done to accomplish the mission.

Plan to Plan. "The cookbook," a manual describing how the planning process is conducted, its time frame, methodology and situation assessment.

Situation Assessment. Analysis of the external and internal environment within which the bank operates.

Strategy. An approach to achieve the objectives necessary to accomplish the bank's mission. A strategy is the answer to questions about how to get where the bank wants to go.

Synergy. The fit between elements so that the whole is greater than the sum of the parts, and the leverage of each element is maximized.

Threat/Opportunity Matrix. A methodology to examine and prioritize bank threats and opportunities, followed by the development of strategies to address those threats and opportunities identified.

Practical Tools for Strategic Planning

The purpose of this section is to present practical tools which can facilitate the selection of the most appropriate strategic position for your thrift within the context of a strategic planning process.

Critical Issues Analysis

An important first step in developing a pragmatic and workable strategic plan is to develop a philosophy or approach to planning that corresponds to the realities of the bank. The approach can range from qualitative to quantitative.

The qualitative planning philosophy stresses the creative aspects of planning. It is generally based upon past experience, the data base, "gut" feel, and management's judgment. Input from other personnel is informal and if any key manager leaves the organization, the process is thrown into disarray. The quantitative, more detail oriented approach, is characterized by formal processes involving large numbers of personnel in periodic exercises designed to quantify innumerable relevant variables and input them into the planning process. This process can limit creative planning and innovative thought and result in mechanical "fill in the blanks."

The critical issues approach to planning combines both qualitative and quantitative methodologies. This approach advocates a concise, creative process to identify the important issues the company will be facing in the next planning period (typically three to five years) and focuses on those key issues. Thus, this approach forces the prioritization of issues and enhances a strategic view as opposed to a detailed operational view of the business. Supplementing the situation analysis data base, brief statements addressing important strategic issues are prepared (see Table 9–1).

Goal Setting

Developing a realistic set of objectives can be one of the most difficult steps in strategic planning. Unrealistic objectives can frustrate staff and disappoint top management. Alternatively, overly conservative objectives decrease staff productivity and may limit performance. Therefore, developing an effective process for setting objectives is critical to the eventual success of the strategic decision-making pro-

Table 9–1: Critical Issues Orientation

◆ Concise

◆ Action oriented

◆ Strategic vs. operational issues

◆ Changes emphasis from mechanistic to creative

187

cess. The procedure set forth below has been used successfully to circumvent traditional goal setting difficulties:

1. Each member of the senior management is asked to prepare a list of ten objectives for their line of business.

2. The chief executive then prepares a similar list of objectives without knowledge of what the staff members have proposed. Likewise, the members of the staff do not have prior knowledge of the manager's objectives.

3. Each member of the line staff presents his or her objectives to the entire staff for discussion. A master list of all of the objectives of the entire group (excluding the CEO) is compiled, after editing out duplications and inconsistencies in objectives.

4. Each member of the staff (excluding the manager) is asked to rank order all of the objectives in the master list. A weighted average of the rankings of the objectives across the entire staff is compiled.

5. The chief executive then presents his or her list of objectives to the staff for discussion and comparison with the composite objectives of the staff.

6. The chief executive then negotiates with the staff to resolve any serious differences between the staff's composite objectives and the CEO's objectives.

7. The CEO makes a final decision in line of business/divisional objectives.

Although this procedure has been used by many organizations, it has some limitations. First, conflicts between the chief executive and staff are bound to arise. Many companies find outside consultants helpful in resolving such conflicts. Second, some important objectives may be eliminated through the weighting process and never be presented. Third, each member of the staff receives an equal vote; this may not be realistic in terms of experience or contribution to the bank. In spite of these limitations, this approach to goal setting has proven effective when the bank line manager provides strong leadership during the process.

In providing this leadership, the CEO should ask his or her staff to provide both general goals (e.g., increase market share) and specific goals (e.g., achieve cross-sell ratio of at least 4.0). The interactive process will ensure that the goals presented are meaningful, reasonable, and challenging, but the manager must ensure that they are consistent with each other and quantifiable, so that they can be integrated into the reward system.

The Market Attractiveness/Business Positioning Matrix

This technique combines external and internal analyses to relate your individual thrift's position to the markets within which you operate. The first step of the analysis is to list relevant factors of market attractiveness. Table 9–2 provides a list of factors any combination of which may fit your definition of an attractive market. Relevant factors for determining an attractive market vary by thrift. For example, if you are a consumer lender and your goal is growth, the high growth, younger, stable markets will be on your attractive segment list; if your goal is stable profitability and low loan losses, offering home equity lines to the older customer segment with lower risk characteristics may be more attractive. Hence, the characteristics of an attractive market will depend on the thrift, its goals, and its mission and business focus.

Having listed these factors, you proceed to assess the market's characteristics and attractiveness. The assessment will be based on your assumptions about the general economic and social environment. It is important to make these underlying assumptions explicit, since a change in these conditions (e.g., risk analysis) may have a dramatic impact on the attractiveness of the market. This information is used to construct a market attractiveness profile for each potential or existing market considered. However, this profile is only part of the analysis and is not sufficient to make strategic decisions involving market entry, market share increase, or withdrawal.

The other element involves your thrift positioning in the market. For example, even though a market may be highly attractive, the bank may have no presence in it, making entry difficult. Conversely, you may be dominant in a declining market, in which case harvesting may be appropriate. Therefore, assessing your positioning within each of the markets is an integral part of the equation. This list in Table 9–2 provides information for assessing bank business position in a particular market. Thus, both market attractiveness and bank position and relative strength within that market are assessed.

Having completed this assessment, you can portray the results on a market attractiveness/business strength matrix (see Figure 9–4). There are distinct strategies associated with each position on the matrix, as illustrated by Figure 9–5. Figure 9–4 illustrates the application of these strategic modes to specific products. This $3-5 billion thrift in a money center area is strong in the small business marketplace, an attractive market for the bank; weak at cross-selling investment services such as annuities or mutual funds, a service they planned on launching; and unsuccessful in its attempts to attract the professional segment to the bank. Consequently, the bank chose to abandon and support C, home equity loans. Annuities and mutual funds were a question mark, yet presented strong potential.

Table 9–2: Factors Contributing to Market Attractiveness and Business Position

Attractiveness of Your Market	Status/Position of Your Bank
MARKET FACTORS	
Size (dollars, units or both)	Your share (in equivalent terms) – absolute and relative
Size of key segments	Your share of key segments – absolute and relative
Growth rate per year:	Trend in market share
Total (past, projected)	Your annual growth rate:
Segments (past, projected)	Total
Diversity of market	Segments
Price sensitivity	
Service sensitivity	
Quality sensitivity	
Image sensitivity	
Technological announcing sensitivity	Diversity of your participation
Convenience sensitivity	Your influence on the market
Customer concentration, market saturation	Concentration of own customers
Stage in "Life Cycle" of each product	Rating in each sensitivity area
Industry profitability	
COMPETITION	
Types of competitors	Where you fit, how you compare in terms of
Size of competitors	product lines, full service concept profitability,
• Number of competitors	marketing capability, financial strength, management
• Trends in number of competitors	
Degree of concentration	Relative quality
Changes in type and mix	Relative price
	Customized products
Entries and exits	
Changes in share	Segments you have entered or left
Substitution by new services/product lines	Your relative share change
Degrees and types of integration	Your vulnerability to new technology
	Your own level of integration
FINANCIAL FACTORS	
Contribution margins	Your margins
Leveraging factors, such as economics of scale	Your scale and experience
and experience	
Barriers to entry and exit (both financial and non-financial)	Barriers to your entry or exit (both financial and
Capacity utilization	non-financial)
Fixed cost or fixed capital intensity	Your capacity utilization

Table continues

Table 9–2: Continued

Attractiveness of Your Market	Status/Position of Your Bank
TECHNOLOGICAL FACTORS	
Maturity and volatility	Your ability to cope with change
Complexity	Depths of your skills
Differentiation	Types of your technological skills
Patents and copyrights	Your patent protection
New services/product lines	Rate of product innovation
SOCIO-POLITICAL FACTORS IN YOUR ENVIRONMENT	
Social attitudes and trends	Your bank's responsiveness and flexibility
	Your bank's ability to cope
Laws and government agency regulations	
Influence with pressure groups and government representatives (e.g. environmentalists)	Your bank's agressiveness
Human factors such as community acceptance	Your bank's relationships
ECONOMIC FACTORS	
GNP:	
Dollars	
Trend	
Inflation Absolute and trend	
Interest rates "	Your interest rate sensitivity
Employment "	Your vulnerability to inflation
Factory output "	
Inventory level "	
Per capital income "	
DEMOGRAPHIC FACTORS	
Fertility rates	
Infant mortality	
Population growth: Total by region	
Population age distribution	
POLITICAL FACTORS	
Hostile or favorable climate	Your risk exposure
Terrorist activity frequency and success	
Government stability	
Overall country risk analysis	

Figure 9-4:
Business Strength/Market Attractiveness Matrix

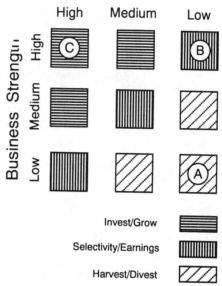

A = Commercial real estate
C = Home equity lines
B = Credit card lending

To this typical thrift, located in a small community in the midwest, commercial real estate is not an attractive market. Home equity lines, on the other hand, are not only perceived attractive but the bank is well positioned to offer them credit cards, however, although attractive due to their high profitability and access to a younger, new customer segment, are difficult to enter and the thrift is currently not well positioned to capture that market.

Figure 9–5:
Business Strength/Market Attractiveness Matrix

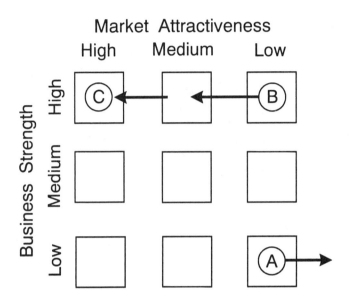

The strategic solution, once the alternatives are clearly mapped out, is obvious: exit the highly risky commercial real estate markets; harvest the home equity line business; and attempt to expand the thrift's know-how of consumer lending into other types of lending such as auto loans (more familiar to a collateral-based lender) or credit cards (unsecured but highly profitable).

The bank finally decided to proceed with this market to leverage their strong retail presence.

Thus, the market attractiveness/business strength approach provides you with a structured method to determine:

◆ What markets you want to get into or out of

◆ Your position within those markets

◆ The strategies associated with that position

◆ Threat/Opportunity Matrix

The Threat/Opportunity matrix presented as Figure 9–6 provides a way of arraying potential threats or opportunities with their relative probabilities of occurrence. A particular event is plotted on a two dimensional matrix—one axis represents the probability that an event will occur within the planning horizon, while the other dimension reflects the impact of that event upon bank earnings.

The first step in the Threat/Opportunity Matrix is to identify the events which will have a major impact on the bank. Then, the probability off occurrence of each event and its potential impact on earnings are estimated given that the bank does not take any action to avoid the threat or capitalize upon the opportunities.

For example, if you visualize Figure 9.6 without arrows, you will see the events that were assessed with no bank action:

Figure 9–6: Threat/Opportunity Matrix

A= Consumer Lending
B= Opening Annuities Market
C= Correspondent Banking
D= Electronic Banking
E= Interstate Banking

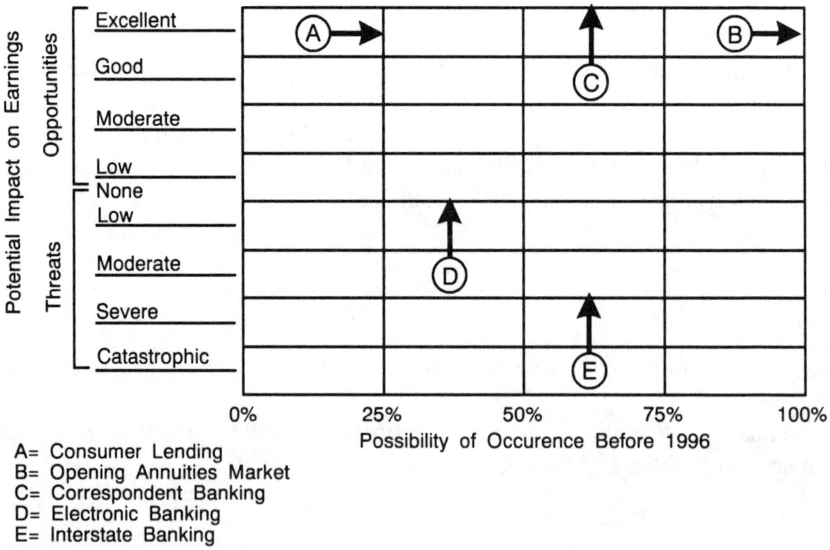

A. The probability of bank entry into consumer lending is very low because of internal resistance to change; at the same time potential profitability is high.

B. The probability of entering the (high potential) annuities market before 1996 is high.

C. Asset securitization through correspondent banking is seen as a medium-potential step available with an average probability of occurrence.

D. Home banking will have a catastrophic impact on the bank and when it is implemented many customers are expected to opt for banks which offer this convenience. It is viewed as having a low probability of occurrence.

E. Interstate branching may result in loss of customers and market share due to enhanced competition. Probability of occurrence before 1996 is perceived to be average.

Once events have been plotted on the Threat/Opportunity Matrix, the bank should consider strategies which will impact either the probability of occurrence or earnings impact (See Figure 9.6, with arrows). In other words, strategies are sought to lessen earnings impact of potential threats or improve the earnings impact of opportunities, as well as increase likelihood of opportunities and decrease that of threats, if feasible.

In some cases, such as examples C, D, and E, the bank cannot change the probability of occurrence. However, the bank can act to improve the potential impact of its earnings by preparing for home banking, augmenting customer relationships to defend against potential interstate competition and broadening the product line offered to correspondents to increase profits. In other cases, such as example A, the bank can design strategies to improve the probability of occurrence to further capitalize on these potential opportunities by ensuring entrance into the promising annuities market and lobbying internally for entering the consumer lending business.

In summary, the Threat/Opportunity Matrix is a tool to discipline and organize your thoughts. It is thought intensive, not paper intensive. The tool prioritizes events to be addressed and provokes thought regarding how to address these events—threats and opportunities—and thus develop strategies. Finally, the matrix provides a picture of what management believes to be the most important factors that are calling for action.

Growth Share Matrix

Each chief executive has a portfolio of products or profit centers and must decide how to allocate resources across that portfolio. The growth share matrix, developed by the Boston Consulting Group, is a tool used in formulating resource allocation strategies, which focuses on cash flow.

To use the matrix, strategic business units (SBUs) in the thrift must first be identified. Ideally, each line of business has the following characteristics:

1. It is a single business or collection of related businesses.

2. It has a distinct mission.

3. It has its own competitors.

4. It has a responsible manager.

5. It consists of one or more program units and functional units.

6. It can benefit from strategic planning.

7. It can be planned independently of the other businesses.

At a bank, where most activities are closely linked at the customer, production, or distribution level, it is often difficult and even impractical to use the SBU concept. However, as the banking industry diversifies into the financial services business, greater applicability of the process may be found. A bank SBU, depending on the circumstances, can be a department, a product line, or sometimes a single product, such as home equity lines, small business lending, mortgage insurance, or securitization.

The next step calls for management to classify all of the SBUs in a way that would reveal their resource allocation merit. This is accomplished by plotting their position on the growth/share matrix (see Figure 9–7).

The circles depict the growth share standings of the bank's various SBUs. The areas of the circles are proportional to the SBU's profitability. The higher an SBU's market share, the higher its cash generating ability. That is because higher market shares appear to be accompanied by higher levels of profitability. On the other hand, the higher the market growth rate, the higher the SBU's cash-using requirements in order for it to grow and maintain its share.

The applicability of the growth/share concept to service businesses is limited. More on this technique can be found in the bibliography list.

Figure 9–7: The BCG Business Portfolio Matrix

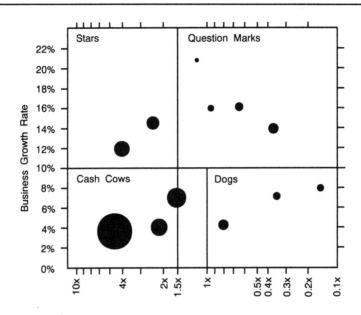

Source: Reprinted from B. Hedley, "Strategies and the Busines Portfolio," *Long Range Planning,* Vol. 10. Copyright 1977, with permission of Pergamon Press Ltd., Headington Hill Hall, Oxford OX3 OBW, UK.

Computer Planning Models

Even a simplified planning model may have more variables than can be depicted on a two-dimensional matrix. To assess the impact of alternative assumption on strategies in more complex situations, computer models are often helpful.

Although planning models came into existence in the early 1960s, their use did not become widespread until the middle 1970s. The advent of computer-based planning models is a direct response to a series of changes with increasing pace, encountered by corporations in the early 1970s. As it became apparent that manual planning systems were not adequate to meet the planning requirements of the ever-changing future, computer planning models have proven to be powerful tools to enable management to cope more effectively with an uncertain future.

A computer-based planning system for a thrift would generally include the following elements:

Planning System. The "plan to plan" for the computer model, it outlines how marketing and production models will be integrated into financial models.

Management Information System. This typically includes the data base, data base system, report generator, and security system. To develop computer planning models, bank financial and economic data and data on relevant markets must be available for easy entry into and access from the system.

Modeling System. This section defines some of the basic terminology used to develop computer planning models, including definition of variables and model specification. Variables are generally classified as output, external, policy, random, and lagged output. Models are specified by formulating definitional and behavioral equations to develop model solutions for output variables given values for the other variables.

Forecasting System. This system allows the model to generate short-term forecasts for market planning models, or other external variables that appear to have a reasonably stable relationship over time.

Econometric Modeling System. This system provides computer simulation capability for evaluating the effects of alternative pricing, advertising, and competitive strategies on sales volume or market share. It also can be used to link market forecasts to national and regional economics.

Computer System. Corporate planning modeling systems may be run either interactively or in a batch, either on the user's in-house computer or on an outside service bureau. Service bureaus and time sharing are often useful for developing the models, but lower cost mini and micro computers have improved systems cost-effectiveness.

Software. A number of languages are available for planning, some created specifically for this purpose, and some more general languages that can be adapted to planning needs. The language to be used and the software to be purchased depends upon a number of factors, including price, flexibility and ease of use.

Development of Bank Products

Bankers have added new products to match the competition or as deregulation has gradually expanded the range of products available. The headlong rush to add new products may not always result in product lines consistent with a bank's strategic objectives or competitive position. This section describes some of the considerations and a process for considering new bank products as part of the strategic planning process. Essentially, the product development process involves answering these strategic questions:

◆ Why offer the product?

◆ What will be the impact of offering the product?

◆ What will be the impact of not offering the product?

◆ How should the new product be developed?

Answers to these questions may involve assumptions or data that are not readily available or ascertainable. In such cases, management may have to provide estimates based on judgment and experience, arrange to have necessary data compiled, or rely upon the experience of other institutions that have offered similar products in similar markets.

Why offer the product? The answer to this question determines the criteria on which the go-ahead decision will be made. A number of objectives may be associated with various products including the following:

◆ Profitability

◆ Cost containment

◆ Customer service

◆ Growth

◆ Market share

◆ Defensive position

◆ Membership needs

◆ Enhanced image

In most cases, numerous objectives will apply. For example, objectives for a credit card operation may involve additional loan growth and income, improved customer access to credit, expanded use of bank services, attraction of new customers and improved competitive position. When multiple objectives are identified, prioritization is important to specify the objectives of primary importance.

Once reasons for wanting to offer the product have been identified, the next step is to study the products potential to realize the stated objectives.

What will be the impact of offering the product? The impact of a new product on bank financial positions, operations, costs, personnel, and customers is uncertain and depends on a number of assumptions which may require analysis that looks at a number of cases, e.g., a worst case, best case, or most probable case.

A product feasibility study should consider the following:

Impact on Customers. Will the proposed product be used by customers?

Estimates of product demand over a period of several years should be prepared. Demand estimates may involve the number of existing members that will use the product, the number of transactions, dollar volume, and/or the number of customers who may be added or lost as a result of the product. Estimates of this type may require judgmental assumptions and hence a number of different demand *scenarios* should be considered. To ensure sufficient facilities to encompass potential growth, demand forecasts should be prepared for a period of at least three to five years.

Profitability, Revenue and Costs. The feasibility study should review the revenue generated by the product and product costs to estimate net income which the product may generate.

A systematic approach to product profitability analysis involves the following steps:

◆ Define the products and product lines. In the case of credit cards, this would involve the credit determination, lending function, collections, transaction processing, i.e., all the activities required to offer the product.

◆ Calculate gross and unit product revenues. revenues should also be computed on a per transaction basis if appropriate.

◆ Perform cost analysis of the product delivery functions.

◆ Analyze the results to determine feasibility and profit improvement potential.

Operations. What facilities, personnel, or other resources will be necessary to offer the product and how much time will be required before the product is available?

The resources required to deliver the product should be listed in as comprehensive a manner as possible. This process is necessary to estimate product costs but is also required to assess the potential impact on the organization. For example, a credit card operation may involve new personnel or computer resources, which in turn may require new physical or computing facilities. As in profitability analysis, the sensitivity of operational requirements to unexpected demand should be considered.

A related issue is excess capacity. How much capacity for growth should be added? A project delivery system that can be expanded only at significant cost and difficulty should be "sized" carefully to avoid unpleasant surprises if growth exceeds expectations.

Marketing. What marketing efforts and resources will be required to inform customers and generate product demand?

Marketing costs may be significant to introduce and promote the product. Such costs should be explicitly considered in the profitability analysis.

Competition. Who is currently providing the product?

Pricing decisions and demand estimates could be generated through a review of financial institutions perceived to be primary competitors in a particular market. The competition's reaction to market entry, if any, should be considered. For example, will bank entry with a lower priced product lead, in turn, to price cutting by competition?

Impact on Other Products. What will be the effect on demand for products currently offered?

Introduction of a new product may contribute to additional demand for other products. For example, a new type of account may encourage customers to use other bank services. Conversely, a new product may reduce demand for products currently offered. A credit card product may substitute for small personal loans. Profiles indicating the numbers and types of products used by customers may be of assistance in exploring potential impacts of this type.

What will be the impact of not offering the product? A product feasibility study may indicate if a new product is not particularly profitable. However, there is a risk of losing customers if a bank does not continue to provide a competitive product line. Thus, bank management should also consider the strategic consequences of not adding a new product.

It may be difficult to estimate the impact of not offering a new product. Market research directed toward a bank's existing customer base can provide one approach for estimating customer and revenue attrition.

How should the new product be developed? The feasibility study will typically review several approaches for developing a new product. Common product development options involve the choice between "making" a new product or buying a new product "off the shelf" from a vendor or another bank. Buying a ready-made bank product may be a cost-effective way of supplementing the existing product line, especially the existing product line, when a new product involves specialized expertise, equipment, or operational considerations. For example, many banks do not have sufficient resources to develop a sophisticated cash management products or a home banking system "from scratch." Such banks wishing to offer these products may purchase or license the technology.

Purchasing a new product is not always preferable to developing a new product in-house. In-house product development allows the bank to tailor product specifications to better meet specific customer needs. In-house product development costs may be defrayed if the new product can be sold or licensed to other financial institutions. Also, internal product development offers the opportunity to link new products to existing products. Product linkages can improve customer services, improve product profitability, and strengthen customer relationships.

Development of Performance Measurement Criteria

Successful implementation of a departmental strategic plan will require development of performance standards to measure progress toward the attainment of strategic objectives and goals. Criteria for measuring performance will vary depending upon the product, service, or activity being evaluated. Performance indices can generally be classified into one of the following types:

◆ *Time.* For example, the time required to process a loan application, open a new account, or address a complaint.

◆ *Physical Units or Events.* For example, the number of credit card applications processed, customer complaints resolved, new accounts added, or number of new business development calls.

◆ *Dollars.* For example, average gross or net revenue on commercial loans, occupancy costs, branch profitability, or cost reductions.

Performance standards involving time, physical units, or events are often preferable to dollar standards because many of the factors which influence costs and revenues are beyond the control of the line manager (e.g., inflation, bank-wide cost of funds, or overhead allocations). In addition, line managers perceive dollar measures as risky and very difficult to anticipate. At the same time, not meeting a dollar target is penalized. However, dollar performance standards implemented through the budgeting process are an important part of internal controls.

The first step in developing performance standards is to determine those standards that relate to key objectives. For example, if growth in commercial loan volume is seen as a primary objective, then a performance standard requiring a specific number of officer calls per week to target market segments could be appropriate. This standard could be accompanied by targets for new loan commitments and a number of referrals to other bank departments.

It is also useful to support this specific target with loan loss targets, as oftentimes rapid growth is accompanied by greater than average losses.

Once the appropriate performance standards have been identified, the actual levels should be determined. If available, historical data can be used to set baseline standards. If historical data is not available, trial standards can be instituted until sufficient performance data have been collected to set base performance standards.

After a performance monitoring system has been put into place, actual performance should be monitored and compared to standards. A variance report (see Figure 9–8) is one way to summarize and compare actual performance to performance standards.

Figure 9–9 provides an example of a form for use in preparing and documentation action plans for strategy implementation. This form, entitled Strategy Summary presents the title, purpose and criteria for strategy selection. The Strategy Summary also contains a format for listing all the actions required to achieve implementation, a time frame for each step's completion, individual responsibility for completing the action, and the strategy. Finally, the form provides for an indication of a go/no-go decision if appropriate. At times it is appropriate to review the strategy prior to completion to decide whether to continue implementation. For example, a strategy to upgrade the bank's data processing capacity will include a feasibility study for the upgrade. Upon completion of the study, the decision may be made to not go ahead with the upgrade due to cost, timing, or other reasons. That evaluation point is a go/no-go decision point.

The second page of the form documents the costs and benefits associated with implementation. These include performance criteria—both financial and nonfinancial—as well as resource requirements for implementation. Resources required

Figure 9–8: Performance Variance Report

DATE

PERFORMANCE STANDARD DESCRIPTION

For Period Ended _____

	Actual Performance	Standard	Actual Variance	% Variance
1.				
2.				
3.				
4.				
5.				
6.				
7.				

For Period Ended _____

Actual Performance	Standard	Actual Variance	Performance Variance

Figure 9-9: Strategy Implementation Form

STRATEGY SUMMARY

DEPARTMENT: _____

NAME OF STRATEGY: _____

STATUS	CRITERIA FOR STRATEGY SELECTION
☐ Existing ☐ Improved ☐ New	☐ To Expoloit a Profit Opportunity. ☐ To Address a Competitive Threat. ☐ To Capitalize on Your Strength ☐ To Reduce Expenses. ☐ Other

STRATEGY SELECTION (why was the strategy selected):

_____

_____

_____

_____

IMPLEMENTATION

Action	Starting & Completion Dates	Person Responsible	Go/No Go Point Decision

could be human, capital, or other departments. Computer, marketing or sales support from other departments should be specified to highlight the fact that they are a necessary requirement for implementation. This entry also becomes useful in finalizing interdepartmental coordination, and in prioritizing support activities such as data processing and marketing.

Table 9–3: Strategy Selection Checklist

A. Is the strategy consistent with environment?

1. Is your strategy consistent with the environment of your bank?

2. Is your strategy acceptable to the major constituents of your bank?

3. Do you really have an honest and accurate appraisal of your competition? Are you underestimating your competition?

4. Does your strategy leave you vulnerable to the power of one major customer?

5. Have you fallen prey to the hockey stick project syndrome?

6. Does your strategy follow that of a strong competitor?

7. Does your strategy pit you against a powerful competitor?

8. Is your market share (present and/or prospective) sufficient to be competitive and make an acceptable profit?

9. If your strategy seeks an enlarged market share is it likely to be stopped by the Antitrust Division of the Department of Justice?

10. Is it possible that other federal government agencies will prevent your achieving the objectives sought by your strategy?

11. Is your strategy legal and in conformance with moral and ethical codes of conduct applicable to your bank?

B. Is the strategy consistent with your internal policies, styles of management, philosophy, and operating procedures?

12. Is your strategy identifiable and understood by all those in the company with a need to know?

13. Is your strategy consistent with the internal strengths, objectives, and policies of your organization?

14. Is the strategy under evaluation divided into substrategies that interrelate properly?

15. Does the strategy under review conflict with other strategies in your company?

16. Does the strategy exploit your strengths and avoid your major weaknesses?

17. Is your organizational structure consistent with your strategy?

18. Is the strategy consistent with the values of top management and other key people in the organization?

C. Is the strategy appropriate in light of your resources?

Money

19. Do you have sufficient capital, or can you get it, to see the strategy through to successful implementation?

20. What will be the financial consequences associated with the allocation of capital to this strategy? What other projects may be denied funding? Are the financial substrategies associated with this funding acceptable?

Physical Plant

21. Is your strategy appropriate with respect to existing and prospective physical plants?

Managerial Resources

22. Are there identifiable available and committed managers to implement the strategy?

D. Are the risks in pursuing the strategy acceptable?

23. Has the strategy been tested with appropriate risk analysis, such as return on investment, sensitivity analysis, the firm's ability and willingness to bear specific risks, etc.?

24. Does your strategy balance the acceptance of minimum risk with the maximum profit potential consistent with your company's resources and prospects?

25. Do you have too much capital and management tied into this strategy?

26. Is the payback period acceptable in light of potential environmental change?

27. Does the strategy take you too far from your current products and markets?

E. Does the strategy fit product life cycle and market strength/market attractiveness situation?

    28. Is the strategy appropriate for the present and prospective position in the market strength/attractiveness matrix?

    29. Does the strategy fit the life cycle of the products involved?

    30. Are you rushing a revolutionary product to market?

    31. Does your strategy involve the production of a new product for a new market? If so, have you really assessed the requirements to implement it successfully?

    32. Does your strategy fit a niche in the market that is not now filled by others? Is this niche likely to remain open to you for a long enough time to return your capital investment plus a required profit?

F. Is the timing proposed implementation correct?

    33. Is the timing of implementation appropriate in light of what is known about market conditions, competition, etc?

G. Are there other important considerations?

    34. Overall, can the strategy be implemented in an efficient and effective fashion?

The strategic planning summary provided in Table 9–4 demonstrates the consistency a plan should have. The mission's components are translated into key

Table 9-4
Strategic Planning Summary

MISSION	KEY OBJECTIVE	STRATEGIES	ACTION PLANS	DEPARTMENT
Anticipate and meet our customers' needs	Identify market needs and meet them	Develop customer calling program	Prepare selected customer list and establish calling procedures	Marketing
	Expand services (both loans and deposits) with market area	Penetrate oil and gas industry	Develop new products targeted at potential oil and gas customers	Commercial lending
		Develop non-customer calling programs	Identify potential customers and establish calling procedures	Marketing
	Maintain image as the number 1 bank in the area by offering the latest, most modern and up-to-date banking services	Pursue ATM installation	Conduct ATM feasibility study	Management
		Increase community involvement	Identify community activities for increased participation	
		Increase board involvement	Develop plans for using board directors to further bank goals	Management
Enhance profitability	Increase loans and deposits within market area	Penetrate oil and gas industry	Develop marketing plan for oil and gas customers	Marketing
		Develop non-customer calling program	Identify potential customers and establish calling procedures	Marketing
	Attain a loan to deposit ratio of approximately 75%	Develop installment loan program	Hire installment loan officer	Commercial lending
	Improve yield on investment portfolio	Develop detailed plan for upgrading bond portfolio yield	Develop portfolio performance benchmarks and monitor portfolio yield	Treasury

objectives. These in turn are matched against strategies designed to achieve the objectives. Finally, action plans are developed to implement each strategy, and the department responsible for implementation is specified.

In addition, external and internal strategic planning flows are depicted in Figures 9–10 and 9–11. These outline the strategic stimuli, both internal and external, which our thrift faces every day, the strategic options available to you in handling the stimuli, and action tools used to do so. Ultimately, the thrift's strategic responses will relate to products, service levels, pricing, linkages, or strategic focus.

For example, when the regulators affected a significant change in the regulatory structure, such as reducing the Qualified Thrift Lender's Test from 70 percent of assets to 65 percent of assets, that had potentially great strategic implications to thrifts. Their response options included positioning for this change, exploiting it, defending against it, or lobbying for/against it. Each response involves a product, service level, linkages, or strategic focus. For example, this reduction in the QTL test expanded thrifts' opportunities in offering more consumer lending related products, more business loans, and other services which do not qualify under QTL (namely, non-residential real estate lending). These options, not available prior to the new rule, implied strategic focus opportunities for thrifts which did not exist before, such as a greater focus on consumer lending, or a full-service community banking operation. It is in this context that inputs from the external and internal environments need to be evaluated and responded to.

In the context of this book, strategic responses are business focus initiatives. They involve the recognition that "business as usual" is no longer an option. Thrift institutions are being deregulated out of business by the marketplace. Their initial strategic niche has shrunk significantly, although it has not been fully eliminated. There is still room for the community mortgage lender. However, that niche cannot support the full range of surviving thrift institutions in the 1990s. As further deregulation unfolds following the last reregulation wave of FIRREA and FIDICIA, thrifts are seeking their future identify.

This book examined in detail three of these strategic alternatives, their definitional characteristics and critical success factors. In addition, the book provides a strategic thinking framework and several tools for each thrift to analyze its own situation and select the strategic niche best suited for it (which may not be included in the three examples explored here). As you, the chief executive, evaluate your options, leverage points and your position in the ever-evolving financial services industry, keep the following guidelines in mind:

1. Plan or be planned for

2. If you don't have a competitive advantage, don't compete

Figure 9-10: Strategic Planning Flow (Internal)

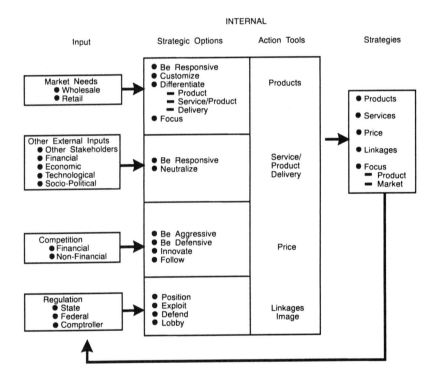

Figure 9–11: Strategic Planning Flow (External)

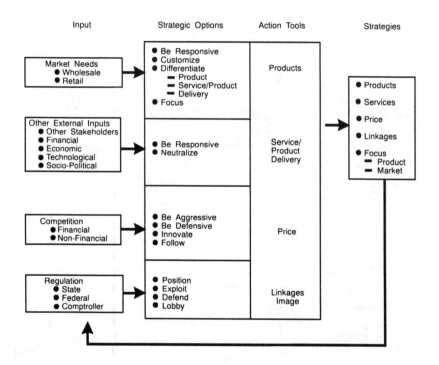

3. No change is not an option

4. See yourself and the world realistically—don't put your rose-colored glasses on.

Conclusion

The thrift industry will not survive as a single industry. Hundreds of individual institutions will survive, however. Their traditional strategy position as a long-term residential real estate lender funded by deposits which are comprised mostly of savings and certificates of deposits can support many strong survivors, yet will no longer be viable for many current industry participants. That change emanated from the nationalization and commoditization of both residential real estate lending and the deposit markets. The unique position historically occupied by the thrift industry due to a monopolistic position sanctified by the regulators has been eliminated.

Consequently, individual institutions need to examine their own strengths and weaknesses and points of leverage in order to identify the strategic niche which will potentially maximize their profitability and franchise value by taking full advantage of their competitive posture and internal strengths.

This book examined three such strategic niches which involve businesses that could extend current strengths: consumer lending, community banking, and mortgage banking. The critical factors of each one of these businesses are different and, therefore, do not present equal likelihood of success to all thrifts. There are other strategic niches that may offer better opportunities to individual thrifts, depending upon their current market position, skill mix, management strength, and ability to change. The mindset that the surviving profitable institutions with a thrift charter should have integrates change and a clear strategic focus into the day-to-day life. A thrift can no longer assume that what worked in the past will work in the future. By the same token, historically successful positions may be viable for some and should not be dismissed off-hand as a death wish or an unviable strategic alternative.

Each institution must examine its own individual situation and candidly assess the viability and long-term potential of current strategic initiatives.

This book offered a framework for that assessment process using practical result-oriented strategic planning tools to evaluate future strategic initiatives and direction. These tools encourage a thought-intensive, not paper-intensive, strategic planning process. They impose discipline on management's thinking and encourage a candid review of the institution's strengths, weaknesses, opportunities, and threats, as well as the potential offered by the strategic niches examined. The tools also provide a methodology to prioritize activities and compare relative attractiveness of each segment and strategic alternative.

In conclusion, the thrift industry will survive, but not as a stand alone industry. Individual institutions will find a business focus that will integrate them into the financial services industry. Those who will do so will avoid the fate of the railroads which refused to recognize that they are in the transportation business. Thrifts are becoming but one segment of the overall financial services industry as it is undergoing a process of homogenization. It is their strategic focus and business concentration that will define their identity, not their charter. Although residential real estate lending may continue to be their core business, it would be that identity they will carry with them into the future, not the thrift charter per se. Those who recognize the fundamental restructuring of the industry and are prepared to take a good look at themselves in the mirror and make the most with what they've got in order to become a successful company in the financial institutions industry will win.

Index

About the Publisher

PROBUS PUBLISHING COMPANY

Probus Publishing Company fills the informational needs of today's business professional by publishing authoritative, quality books on timely and relevant topics, including:

- Investing
- Futures/Options Trading
- Banking
- Finance
- Marketing and Sales
- Manufacturing and Project Management
- Personal Finance, Real Estate, Insurance and Estate Planning
- Entrepreneurship
- Management

Probus books are available at quantity discounts when purchased for business, educational or sales promotional use. For more information, please call the Director, Corporate/Institutional Sales at 1-800-PROBUS-1, or write:

Director, Corporate/Institutional Sales
Probus Publishing Company
1925 N. Clybourn Avenue
Chicago, Illinois 60614
FAX (312) 868-6250